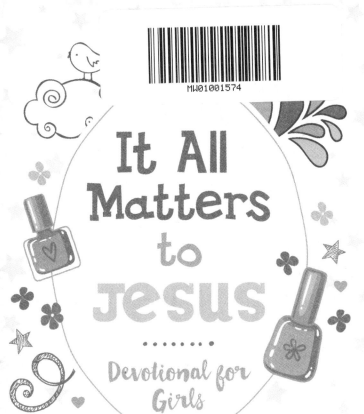

It All Matters to Jesus

Devotional for Girls

It All Matters to Jesus

Devotional for Girls

Mean Girls, Manicures,
and Mondays. . .
He Cares about It All

JoAnne Simmons

BARBOUR BOOKS
An Imprint of Barbour Publishing, Inc.

Dedication:
To my parents, who raised me to know and love Jesus, and to my in-laws for doing the same for my husband. Thank you!

And to Doug and Jodi and Lilly. You make life so full of love and fun.

Acknowledgments:
Adelie, Ashley, Aubrey, Emma, Hannah, Kassadee, Sara, Sarah, and Wyndham—your honest answers were a huge help while I was writing this book. Thank you so much!

© 2016 by Barbour Publishing, Inc.

Print ISBN 978-1-63058-933-2

eBook Editions:
Adobe Digital Edition (.epub) 978-1-63409-749-9
Kindle and MobiPocket Edition (.prc) 978-1-63409-751-2

Scripture quotations marked NLT are taken from the *Holy Bible*. New Living Translation copyright© 1996, 2004, 2007 by Tyndale House Foundation. Used by permission of Tyndale House Publishers, Inc. Carol Stream, Illinois 60188. All rights reserved.

Scripture quotations marked CEV are from the Contemporary English Version, Copyright © 1995 by American Bible Society. Used by permission.

Scripture quotations marked ESV are from The Holy Bible, English Standard Version®, copyright © 2001 by Crossway Bibles, a publishing ministry of Good News Publishers. Used by permission. All rights reserved.

Scripture quotations marked NIV are taken from the HOLY BIBLE, NEW INTERNATIONAL VERSION®. NIV®. Copyright © 1973, 1978, 1984, 2011 by Biblica, Inc.™ Used by permission. All rights reserved worldwide.

Scripture quotations marked NKJV are taken from the New King James Version®. Copyright © 1982 by Thomas Nelson, Inc. Used by permission. All rights reserved.

Scripture quotations marked NASB are taken from the New American Standard Bible, © 1960, 1962, 1963, 1968, 1971, 1972, 1973, 1977, 1995 by The Lockman Foundation. Used by permission.

Published by Barbour Books, an imprint of Barbour Publishing, Inc., P.O. Box 719, Uhrichsville, Ohio 44683, www.barbourbooks.com.

Our mission is to publish and distribute inspirational products offering exceptional value and biblical encouragement to the masses.

Member of the
Evangelical Christian
Publishers Association

Printed in the United States of America.
05301 0216 DP

Contents

Introduction

Okay, first thing: stop right now, wherever you're reading this book—are you in a favorite reading spot? Is it upside down on a beanbag chair, or snuggled with a ginormous pillow on the floor, or propped up on your bed, or crammed into an empty cupboard with a flashlight? The empty cupboard was one of my favorite reading spots when I was about your age. The roof of my house was, too—seriously!—but I do *not* recommend that to anyone else. I'm lucky I didn't break my neck.

Anyway, you need to get one thing straight from the start of this book: the bottom line is that YOU matter to Jesus. So *very* much so that He left a pretty posh place as God in heaven to come down to earth as a baby, live a human life, and then suffer and die a nasty death—but rose from the dead (yay!)—all so He could make a way for you to be with Him in a perfect paradise forever. That's kind of a big deal, don't you think? And if someone loves you that much—and He totally does!—then every single thing in your life is important to Jesus as well. Mean girls, manicures, Mondays. . . whatever.

If it's something that matters to you—good or bad—it matters to Jesus.

How Much Is All—
And How Much Does It All Matter?

Raise your hand if you like math. I'm sitting hard on my hands because I completely *don't*, but I sure hope some of you do because the world needs lots of people who are great at math.

Whether you like numbers or not, can you count to *all*?

That's like asking if you can count to infinity. You just can't do it. Well, you could try, but then you'd spend the rest of your life counting and you'd still never reach the end because (duh!) it's infinity—and who wants to count forever, no matter how much you like numbers?

The title of this book says it all matters to Jesus, emphasis on *all*. That means there is no number limit to what matters to God, and there are no limits on the types of things that matter to God.

If you're not a number lover, then maybe you're a word lover, and you like dictionaries. If you check the dictionary, you'll find definitions of *all* include "the whole, entire, total amount, quantity, or extent of" and "every" and "any whatever." That pretty much covers every single thing we could think of, right? There is *nothing* that matters to us that does not matter to God.

And it's not true just because it's here in this book; it's true because *God's* book, His Word, the Bible, says it's true. Check out these verses:

First Peter 5:7 (NLT) says, "Give all your worries and cares to God, for he cares about you." Does it say just our big worries? No. It says *all*.

In Psalms we read, "Our LORD, we belong to you. We tell you what worries us, and you won't let us fall" (Psalm 55:22 CEV). We have all sorts of things that worry us, from superstressful things to things not quite so serious, but we can tell them *all* to God, and He won't let us down about them.

And no matter what, we can totally trust that "God will supply every need of yours according to his riches in glory in Christ Jesus" (Philippians 4:19 ESV). Every need, every worry, every fear, every problem, every frustration, every anger, every thought. It all matters to Jesus.

Every joy does, too.

Your worries and problems aren't the only things that matter to God. The happy things in your life—joy over getting a new pet, or excitement over an upcoming birthday party for a friend, or an accomplishment like finally sticking that landing in gymnastics—all those types of things matter to Him, as well. He wants to share in your joy, and He wants you to thank and praise Him in all things, just like these verses say:

The Lord is my strength and shield.
I trust him with all my heart.
He helps me, and my heart is filled with joy.
I burst out in songs of thanksgiving.

PSALM 28:7 NLT

Shout for joy to the Lord, all the earth.
Worship the Lord with gladness;
come before him with joyful songs.

PSALM 100:1-2 NIV

Don't worry about anything; instead,
pray about everything. Tell God what you need,
and thank him for all he has done.

PHILIPPIANS 4:6 NLT

And we know that for those who love God all
things work together for good, for those who
are called according to his purpose.

ROMANS 8:28 ESV

So now you might be wondering how much the things in your life, good or bad, matter to God. Just a little bit? Or a lot? The best way to answer that is to focus on how much God loves you. When someone really loves you, then every single aspect of your life, big or small, matters to that person in a big way. And God sure does love you in a *ginormous* way. You can't ever really wrap your mind around it, actually, but you can keep coming back to the following verses about God's love, reading them and memorizing them to help you remember just how much every detail of your life matters to God.

But God shows his love for us in that while
we were still sinners, Christ died for us.
ROMANS 5:8 ESV

For I am sure that neither death nor life, nor angels
nor rulers, nor things present nor things to come,
nor powers, nor height nor depth, nor anything else
in all creation, will be able to separate us from the
love of God in Christ Jesus our Lord.
ROMANS 8:38–39 ESV

*For as high as the heavens are above the earth, so great
is his steadfast love toward those who fear him.*

PSALM 103:11 ESV

*And may you have the power to understand, as all God's
people should, how wide, how long, how high, and how
deep his love is. May you experience the love of Christ,
though it is too great to understand fully.*

EPHESIANS 3:18-19 NLT

*This is real love—not that we loved God, but that he loved
us and sent his Son as a sacrifice to take away our sins.*

1 JOHN 4:10 NLT

*How great is God's love for all who worship him?
Greater than the distance between heaven and earth!*

PSALM 103:11 CEV

*For God so loved the world that he gave his one
and only Son, that whoever believes in him
shall not perish but have eternal life.*

JOHN 3:16 NIV

And if there's any doubt left in your brain about how much God cares about any and every little detail of your life, then think about something for a moment. Do you think you could ever count all the hairs on your pretty head? They won't go to infinity, of course, but still—what a long and boring task that would be! I'm sure you can think of much more fun things to do like baking cookies with your BFF and eating gobs of chocolate chip cookie dough. (Will you save me some? Yum!)

God has done it, though. He cares so much about every detail of your life that He's counted the exact number of hairs on your head. That's pretty detailed.

You are *extremely* loved by God, and *everything* about you matters to Him.

Aren't two sparrows sold for only a penny? But your Father knows when any one of them falls to the ground. Even the hairs on your head are counted. So don't be afraid! You are worth much more than many sparrows.
MATTHEW 10:29-31 CEV

It All Matters to Jesus

❋ Every worry you have matters to Jesus.

❋ Every problem you face matters to Jesus.

❋ Every fear that scares you matters to Jesus.

❋ Every frustration that bothers you matters to Jesus.

❋ Every anger you feel matters to Jesus.

❋ Every sorrow you suffer matters to Jesus.

❋ Every thought you think matters to Jesus.

❋ Every joy you experience matters to Jesus.

❋ Every accomplishment you achieve matters to Jesus.

❋ Even the number of hairs on your head matters to Jesus.

Can't Live with 'Em, Can't Live without 'Em

It's true—your family will absolutely drive you crazy sometimes, maybe even *a lot* of the time. Sometimes we feel like we just can't live with them anymore, but we sure can't live without them, either! Maybe your little brother constantly messes with your stuff—even though you've made clear it's off-limits. (Didn't he see the huge sign on your door to **KEEP OUT**?) Maybe your teenage sister just doesn't understand you're not trying to bother her; you just think she's supercool and you want to know all about her. (Well, okay, maybe you shouldn't have been sneaking to read all the texts on her phone.)

Maybe you don't have siblings, but your parents are always on your case about homework or music practice when you just want to chill. Maybe your parents are divorced and you're tired of shuffling back and forth and being stuck in the middle.

Or [insert your own stressful family situation here]. Maybe it's none or all of the above, but we all have ways that our family members make us want to scream. And crazy or not, they're the people in our lives who've always got our backs, the people we love the very most, the people God has purposefully placed us with.

So, does Jesus care about your family? Does He care if you fight with your siblings? Does He care that it's hard to obey your parents sometimes? Does He care about the things that cause worry and stress and pain in your family? Does He care when you're missing your cousins you only get to see on Thanksgiving? Yes, yes, yes, and yes!

God's Word says in 1 Timothy 5:8 (CEV), "People who don't take care of their relatives, and especially their own families, have given up their faith. They are worse than someone who doesn't have faith in the Lord." Those are strong words, and they make it pretty clear how important family is to Jesus and how important our family should be to us.

So, if you have siblings, how's that going? Do you fight a little or a lot? What ways could you work harder to get along with them? Start by looking for more ways to show love and respect for them.

If a little brother wants to be in your stuff, try to find some extra time to share your things with him. He might just want some attention from you. And if your sister wants you to stop bugging her, try talking things out and telling her why she's so fascinating to you.

Things won't ever be perfect, and your siblings will hurt your feelings and you'll both pick fights at times. But look up 1 Corinthians 13 in your Bible and work harder at loving them in the way those verses talk about love. Don't get upset too easily, and be quick to forgive and forget. God will bless your efforts for trying to do things His way, living in peace and love with your family members. And remember, don't ever stop asking for His help!

Here are some more excellent verses to encourage you in getting along with your siblings:

Ask God to bless everyone who mistreats you. Ask him to bless them and not to curse them. When others are happy, be happy with them, and when they are sad, be sad. Be friendly with everyone. Don't be proud and feel that you are smarter than others. Make friends with ordinary people. Don't mistreat someone who has mistreated you. But try to earn the respect of others, and do your best to live at peace with everyone.
ROMANS 12:14–18 CEV

Now, your parents. . .how well do you get along with them? I know it sometimes seems like they never get off your back. There are so many chores and homework assignments and a bazillion times when you have to be patient or on your best behavior. You probably wonder sometimes, *Why can't I just do whatever I want?* But stop and think about all that your parents are doing for you. There's a lot of work and responsibility that goes into keeping you fed and clothed and learning and healthy and safe—and I bet you do have tons of fun in the midst of all that, too, because your parents love you and want to give you nice things and good experiences. Be sure you show not just obedience and respect for your parents, but love and appreciation, too. The Bible has a *lot* to say about how to treat your parents. . . .

"Honor your father and your mother,
that your days may be long upon the land
which the L<small>ORD</small> your God is giving you."
E<small>XODUS</small> 20:12 <small>NKJV</small>

"Each of you must show great respect
for your mother and father."
L<small>EVITICUS</small> 19:3 <small>NLT</small>

My children, listen when your father corrects you.
Pay attention and learn good judgment.
P<small>ROVERBS</small> 4:1 <small>NLT</small>

*Obey the teaching of your parents—always keep it
in mind and never forget it. Their teaching will guide
you when you walk, protect you when you sleep,
and talk to you when you are awake.*
PROVERBS 6:20-22 CEV

*A wise child brings joy to a father;
a foolish child brings grief to a mother.*
PROVERBS 10:1 NLT

*Children with good sense accept correction from their
parents, but stubborn children ignore it completely.*
PROVERBS 13:1 CEV

*Don't be a fool and disobey your parents.
Be smart! Accept correction.*
PROVERBS 15:5 CEV

*Pay attention to your father, and don't neglect your
mother when she grows old. Invest in truth and wisdom,
discipline and good sense, and don't part with them.
Make your father truly happy by living right and
showing sound judgment. Make your parents proud,
especially your mother.*
PROVERBS 23:22-25 CEV

Sometimes you might have a major worry for a family member—do you have a loved one who is sick? Maybe an aunt who's fighting cancer or a grandparent who has to live in a nursing home? Jesus cares so much about them, and He is working on a place for us where there will never be any more pain and sickness and suffering.

Then I saw "a new heaven and a new earth," for the first heaven and the first earth had passed away, and there was no longer any sea. I saw the Holy City, the new Jerusalem, coming down out of heaven from God, prepared as a bride beautifully dressed for her husband. And I heard a loud voice from the throne saying, "Look! God's dwelling place is now among the people, and he will dwell with them. They will be his people, and God himself will be with them and be their God. 'He will wipe every tear from their eyes. There will be no more death' or mourning or crying or pain, for the old order of things has passed away." He who was seated on the throne said, "I am making everything new!"

REVELATION 21:1–5 NIV

If you have loved ones who are suffering, do you know if they've accepted Jesus as their Savior? If not, think of ways you could share His love and the Gospel with them. (If you need help with this, go to page 25 on how to be sure you have Jesus as your BFF.)

It All Matters to Jesus

❀ Your family matters to Jesus.

❀ Giving time and attention to a little sibling matters to Jesus.

❀ Respecting an older sibling's stuff and space matters to Jesus.

❀ Obeying your parents, even when it's hard, matters to Jesus.

❀ Your family members who are sick matter to Jesus.

❀ Your family's financial needs matter to Jesus.

❀ Missing your family who are far away matters to Jesus.

❀ Appreciating and showing love to your family matters to Jesus.

❀ Forgiveness matters to Jesus.

❀ Taking care of each other matters to Jesus.

BFFs and Bullies and Everyone in Between

Who's your BFF? Do you have just one or a whole bunch? Or maybe you're wishing you could find one. Well, before we go any further, don't ever forget who wants to be your #1, Top-of-the-List, Best Friend Forever—

Jesus.

Just so we have this clear, have you asked Him to be your BFF? If you haven't, do you know how? It's so simple and fantastic to accept His love and forgiveness and ask Him to be your Savior and your very best friend. If you never have, then pray a prayer like this right now:

Dear God, I need You. I know that I mess up and do the wrong thing, but I believe Jesus died on the cross for my sins, and then He rose again and is alive right now. Please forgive me for all my mistakes and be my Savior. Please be my best friend forever and help me to follow You! Thank You for loving me and helping me. Thank You that everything about me matters to You. In Jesus' name, amen.

(Check out these scriptures to help you understand— John 3:16, Romans 3:23, Romans 6:23, Romans 5:8, Romans 10:9–10.)

When Jesus is your BFF, He wants to help you in all your other friendships, too. Have you had a fight with a friend recently? Has someone you thought was a good friend been ignoring you lately? Has a friend started acting so differently that you're not even sure you want to be friends anymore? Has a close friend moved away and you miss that friend terribly?

All these things matter to Jesus.

Or maybe you're blessed and nothing is going wrong with your friends right now, and you are thrilled to have one awesome BFF or maybe more than one! Great! Jesus wants us to have good friends, get along with them, love them, and live in peace with them. Check out these verses from His Word:

A friend loves at all times.
PROVERBS 17:17 NIV

There are "friends" who destroy each other,
but a real friend sticks closer than a brother.
PROVERBS 18:24 NLT

As iron sharpens iron,
so a friend sharpens a friend.
PROVERBS 27:17 NLT

The heartfelt counsel of a friend
is as sweet as perfume and incense.
PROVERBS 27:9 NLT

Two are better than one, because they have a good return
for their labor: If either of them falls down, one can help
the other up. But pity anyone who falls and has no one
to help them up. Also, if two lie down together, they will
keep warm. But how can one keep warm alone? Though
one may be overpowered, two can defend themselves.
A cord of three strands is not quickly broken.
ECCLESIASTES 4:9-12 NIV

Unfortunately, things do go wrong with friends sometimes because we're all human and none of us is perfect—no matter how much we wish that were true.

Sometimes friends will make you feel left out and lonely. When that happens, talk it out with a parent or other trusted grown-up and see if there are ways you can work it out with that friend. And always remember that God has said, "Never will I leave you; never will I forsake you" (Hebrews 13:5 NIV). If there are times when you feel left out by friends, use that time to get closer to God. Let Him show you how much He loves you by spending extra time reading your Bible and listening to music that praises Him. You can also use the time to find ways to help others more, and you might be surprised at how God brings new friends into your life.

If you're not being left out, be thankful, and be careful not to leave someone else out. Be sensitive to how other friends feel, and find ways to include them if you think they're feeling like an outsider, whether it's at school or at church or on the playground or during a dance class or a team sport.

Do you feel like your friends are always getting you into trouble or pressuring you to do things that you know you shouldn't? Are there boys wanting to be more than just friends, or other girls pressuring you to be more than just friends with a boy? Then here's the deal: you absolutely need to make some new friends and let the troublemakers go.

The Bible says in 1 Corinthians 15:33 (CEV). "Don't fool yourselves. Bad friends will destroy you."

And in Proverbs 13:20 (CEV) it says, "Wise friends make you wise, but you hurt yourself by going around with fools."

Do you have friends who pick on you or tease too much—or maybe they're not friends at all but downright bullies? Don't ever be afraid to get help from a parent, teacher, or other trusted grown-up in cases like this (no matter how much the bully threatens to make you miserable if you do), and remember that God sees and knows the hurt done to you. His Word says this:

Never take revenge. Leave that to the righteous anger of God. For the Scriptures say, "I will take revenge; I will pay them back," says the LORD. Instead, "If your enemies are hungry, feed them. If they are thirsty, give them something to drink. In doing this, you will heap burning coals of shame on their heads." Don't let evil conquer you, but conquer evil by doing good.
ROMANS 12:19-21 NLT

Sometimes you've done the best you can, and a friend still hurts or betrays you or bullies you too much—and you finally just have to let that person go. Jesus knows these things will happen. He cares about your hurts, and He cares about your knowing that He is the one true friend who will never let you down.

With Jesus as your Savior, remember your purpose here on earth is to live in relationship with Him and share His love. Do your best to be loving and kind to everyone who comes into your life, for whatever time you get to count them as a friend, confident that nothing and no one can ever take away your greatest friend of all—Jesus.

God loves you and has chosen you as his own special people. So be gentle, kind, humble, meek, and patient. Put up with each other, and forgive anyone who does you wrong, just as Christ has forgiven you. Love is more important than anything else. It is what ties everything completely together.
COLOSSIANS 3:12–14 CEV

It All Matters to Jesus

❃ Being your #1, Top-of-the-List BFF matters to Jesus.

❃ Having good friends matters to Jesus.

❃ Staying away from troublesome friends matters to Jesus.

❃ When you feel left out, it matters to Jesus.

❃ Including others and being a good friend matters to Jesus.

❃ When you feel bullied, it matters to Jesus.

❃ When you lose a friend, it matters to Jesus.

❃ Being kind to those who are unkind to you matters to Jesus.

❃ Not seeking revenge matters to Jesus.

❃ Drawing closer to Him when you feel alone matters to Jesus.

Everything You're Thinking About

Isn't it incredible that God knows *everything*? Especially that He knows your every thought. How can He keep track of the thoughts of so many people in the world? It's kind of mind-boggling, huh? But it's true! Read this beautiful psalm:

You have looked deep into my heart, LORD,
and you know all about me.
You know when I am resting or when I am working,
and from heaven you discover my thoughts.

You notice everything I do and everywhere I go.
Before I even speak a word, you know what I will say,
and with your powerful arm you protect me
from every side. I can't understand all of this!
Such wonderful knowledge is far above me.

Where could I go to escape from your Spirit
or from your sight? If I were to climb up
to the highest heavens, you would be there.
If I were to dig down to the world of the dead
you would also be there.

Suppose I had wings
like the dawning day and flew across the ocean.

33

*Even then your powerful arm would
guide and protect me.*

*Or suppose I said, "I'll hide in the dark until night comes
to cover me over." But you see in the dark because
daylight and dark are all the same to you.*

*You are the one who put me together inside my mother's
body, and I praise you because of the wonderful way you
created me. Everything you do is marvelous!
Of this I have no doubt.*

*Nothing about me is hidden from you! I was secretly
woven together deep in the earth below, but with your own
eyes you saw my body being formed. Even before I was
born, you had written in your book everything I would do.*

*Your thoughts are far beyond my understanding,
much more than I could ever imagine. I try to
count your thoughts, but they outnumber
the grains of sand on the beach.*

PSALM 139:1–18 CEV

Wow! Isn't it awesome that the God of the universe
knows you so well and loves you so much?

Since God knows everything about you, even the thoughts that you think, they obviously matter to Him—and it should matter to you whether your thoughts please Him or not. Here's what the Bible says to think about:

And now, dear brothers and sisters, one final thing. Fix your thoughts on what is true, and honorable, and right, and pure, and lovely, and admirable. Think about things that are excellent and worthy of praise.
PHILIPPIANS 4:8 NLT

Let's stop and do a little brain scan—you'll need some aluminum foil, a lightbulb, and some electrical wire. . .just kidding. We'll leave that kind of thing to the doctors and scientists, and I'm pretty sure they use much more sophisticated equipment.

Seriously, though, do your thoughts match up with that scripture? Hopefully a lot of the time they do, but probably not always. It's tough to always think positively, especially when so many things are going wrong all around you, and especially when you forget that God is listening to your thoughts. The good news is, you can train your brain to do better.

Every time your thoughts start to stray toward things that are false or negative or sinful or hateful or full of complaining, you can think of this verse and ask God to help you focus on good things—like the truth in His Word, the ways He has helped you in the past, the blessings in your life, and the promises of God and His SUPERSIZED love for you!

One verse that's so easy to memorize and so very helpful for training your brain is Isaiah 26:3 (NLT)—"You will keep in perfect peace all who trust in you, all whose thoughts are fixed on you!"

Picture your favorite animal at the zoo. Now picture it going totally nutso when a zookeeper tries to settle it into its new exhibit. Wild, right?

Your thoughts don't have to be untamable, like a wild animal that can't be controlled. You can *choose* to train your brain not to dwell on the bad but focus on the good. This doesn't mean you have to pretend the hard things don't exist. You don't have to step out of reality when bad things happen. But you can learn to never let those negatives take over your head!

Here are some more great verses to help you choose good thoughts:

Let God change the way you think. Then you will know how to do everything that is good and pleasing to him.
ROMANS 12:2 CEV

*Think about the things of heaven,
not the things of earth.*
COLOSSIANS 3:2 NLT

"Love the Lord your God with all your heart and with all your soul and with all your mind."
MATTHEW 22:37 ESV

Let my words and my thoughts be pleasing to you, LORD, because you are my mighty rock and my protector.
PSALM 19:14 CEV

Do your parents ever tell you to watch your attitude or that you need an attitude adjustment? Your thoughts are what shape your attitude, and your attitude matters to Jesus.

What would your reaction be to this scenario: You've been looking forward all week to a Friday night out with just your mom and your BFF to see a new movie you've been waiting on FOR.EV.ER. But then your baby sister gets sick and is vomiting all over the house, and your mom cancels on your friend and the movie.

Ugh! You can choose to think about how bummed you are, how disgusting vomit is, how you're probably going to have to help clean up the mess and probably get sick, too, how everything is always about the baby, and how unfair life is. And all those thoughts are going to make your attitude just as stinky as all the puke—and probably get you into trouble with your parents if you add a bad attitude to an already tough situation.

Or you could say, "Yep, this is a bummer." It's fine to admit it! But then you can choose to think good thoughts—how much you love your baby sister and you're sorry she got sick, how much you love your mom and that she'd appreciate a cheerful helper cleaning up all the puke mess, and how there's always another weekend when you can plan a fun movie night with a friend. And that will make your attitude a good one, which pleases God. . .and will likely earn you some bonus points with your parents. Win, win, win!

It All Matters to Jesus

❀ Thinking about what is true matters to Jesus.

❀ Thinking about what is honorable matters to Jesus.

❀ Thinking about what is right matters to Jesus.

❀ Thinking about what is pure matters to Jesus.

❀ Thinking about what is lovely matters to Jesus.

❀ Thinking about what is admirable matters to Jesus.

❀ Thinking about things that are excellent and worthy of praise matters to Jesus.

❀ Keeping your thoughts fixed on God and His promises matters to Jesus.

❀ Your attitude toward a disappointing situation matters to Jesus.

❀ Training your brain to refocus when you are thinking negatively matters to Jesus.

What Goes In

Do you have a grandma or maybe another older loved one to make warm, fuzzy memories with? I sure hope so. A favorite memory I have of my "Mema," who is now in heaven, is of a song she used to sing with me called "O, Be Careful Little Eyes." If you were to Google it right now, you might roll your eyes at the old-fashioned music videos you'll find, but the message of it is still relevant and valuable, a reminder that what you see and hear matters to Jesus.

Another song I remember that I used to listen to on these crazy old things called cassette tapes (ask your mom and dad about them) was called the "Computer Song" that went like this: "Input, output, what goes in is what comes out. Input, output, that is what it's all about. Input, output, your mind is a computer whose input, output, daily you must choose."

Catchy, huh? LOL!

The point is, what you feed your brain and your heart—the things you watch on TV and the Internet, the types of books and magazines and blogs you read, the Facebook posts and tweets you follow, the type of music you listen to, the video games you play— might just seem like harmless entertainment and socializing, but they are much more than that. They totally affect what comes out of you, too. They affect your beliefs and your words and your attitudes and your actions. And everything that "goes in" matters *a lot* to Jesus. He wants you to fill yourself up with good stuff.

Check out the verses on the next page:

Your eyes are the lamp for your body. When your eyes are good, you have all the light you need. But when your eyes are bad, everything is dark. So be sure that your light isn't darkness. If you have light, and nothing is dark, then light will be everywhere, as when a lamp shines brightly on you.

LUKE 11:34-36 CEV

I will not look with approval on anything that is vile. I hate what faithless people do; I will have no part in it. The perverse of heart shall be far from me; I will have nothing to do with what is evil.

PSALM 101:3-4 NIV

Put everything to the test. Accept what is good and don't have anything to do with evil.

1 THESSALONIANS 5:21-22 CEV

I pray that God, who gives peace, will make you completely holy. And may your spirit, soul, and body be kept healthy and faultless until our Lord Jesus Christ returns.

1 THESSALONIANS 5:23 CEV

"Bad company corrupts good character." Think carefully about what is right, and stop sinning.

1 CORINTHIANS 15:33-34 NLT

So, what should you put in? First off, fill yourself up with God's Word. Spend time in it, not just at church or Sunday school, but *daily*. It's our guidebook for life, and it's our map to make our way closer and closer to Jesus until we can be with Him forever.

Here are some awesome verses to encourage you to study and memorize and live by God's Word:

All Scripture is breathed out by God and profitable for teaching, for reproof, for correction, and for training in righteousness, that the man of God may be complete, equipped for every good work.

2 Timothy 3:16–17 esv

"This Book of the Law shall not depart from your mouth, but you shall meditate on it day and night, so that you may be careful to do according to all that is written in it. For then you will make your way prosperous, and then you will have good success."

Joshua 1:8 esv

And the Scriptures were written to teach
and encourage us by giving us hope.
ROMANS 15:4 CEV

For the word of God is alive and powerful. It is
sharper than the sharpest two-edged sword, cutting
between soul and spirit, between joint and marrow.
It exposes our innermost thoughts and desires.
HEBREWS 4:12 NLT

With my whole heart I seek you; let me not wander
from your commandments! I have stored up your
word in my heart, that I might not sin against you.
PSALM 119:10–11 ESV

"Heaven and earth will pass away,
but my words will not pass away."
MATTHEW 24:35 ESV

Your word is a lamp for my feet,
a light on my path.
PSALM 119:105 NIV

I'm not saying that if you like a popular non-Christian song on the radio, it's always a bad thing, or that every single book you read has to have a Christian message. You don't have to be out of touch with the reality of the world around you or watch only religious movies and TV or can't ever enjoy a song that doesn't have lyrics about God. My point is, what are you continually filling your mind with, and what are you letting affect you and your actions and testimony as a Christian?

Remember the verse we looked at earlier?

Finally, my friends, keep your minds on whatever is true, pure, right, holy, friendly, and proper. Don't ever stop thinking about what is truly worthwhile and worthy of praise.
PHILIPPIANS 4:8 CEV

Here's the deal—if your heart is full of God's Word and you are walking closely with Jesus, you simply have to ask Him to help you be careful and smart about the movies, TV, books, music, etc., that you put into your life. And when you have the Holy Spirit in you, He will help you be attracted to what is good for you and avoid what is bad for you.

Keep this verse as a guide:

Let the message about Christ, in all its richness, fill your lives. Teach and counsel each other with all the wisdom he gives. Sing psalms and hymns and spiritual songs to God with thankful hearts. And whatever you do or say, do it as a representative of the Lord Jesus, giving thanks through him to God the Father.
COLOSSIANS 3:16-17 NLT

Fill your brain and your heart and your life with Jesus and His Word, and remember that everything that goes into your head and your heart matters to Him.

It All Matters to Jesus

❀ The music you listen to matters to Jesus.

❀ The books you read matter to Jesus.

❀ The websites you visit matter to Jesus.

❀ The magazines you read matter to Jesus.

❀ The blogs you read matter to Jesus.

❀ The movies you watch matter to Jesus.

❀ The TV shows you watch matter to Jesus.

❀ Everything you put into your head and your heart matters to Jesus.

❀ Asking for God's help in choosing what to put in your mind matters to Jesus.

❀ Filling up on God's Word matters to Jesus.

What Comes Out— Your Words

It's a big deal when a baby starts talking. Have you asked your mom or dad what your first few words were? Were you a quiet toddler or a little chatterbox? Your parents might have recorded videos from when you first started talking and other fun times when you were smaller. Maybe you can plan a home movie night sometime where the star of the show is you! (Don't forget the popcorn!)

Our words are always a big deal to Jesus. Look at this scripture:

All of us do many wrong things. But if you can control your tongue, you are mature and able to control your whole body. By putting a bit into the mouth of a horse, we can turn the horse in different directions. It takes strong winds to move a large sailing ship, but the captain uses only a small rudder to make it go in any direction. Our tongues are small too, and yet they brag about big things. It takes only a spark to start a forest fire! The tongue is like a spark. It is an evil power that dirties the rest of the body and sets a person's entire life on fire with flames that come from hell itself. All kinds of animals, birds, reptiles, and sea creatures can be tamed and have been tamed. But our tongues get out of control.

*They are restless and evil, and always spreading
deadly poison. My dear friends, with our tongues
we speak both praises and curses.
We praise our Lord and Father, and we curse people who
were created to be like God, and this isn't right.*

JAMES 3:2-10 CEV

There's so much to ponder in those verses, but the
bottom line is that your words are very powerful. They
can do a lot of good, and they can do a lot of bad—and
they are very hard to control.

Think about how easy it is to say disrespectful things to your parents or quickly respond with "no"—and then all of a sudden you're in trouble for disobeying. Or how often you "vent" in frustration, and suddenly all these ugly words are coming out of your mouth. Or when a sibling or friend upsets you and in no time you're yelling hateful and hurtful words. Our words are so tied to what we're feeling—mad, sad, frustrated, whatever—and we often let them spew without thinking. The emotions come and go, but the words will be remembered.

Do yourself a huge favor while you are young and get in the supersmart habit of controlling what you say. I'm guessing you don't like to be called immature, right? Do you know a way you can start being really mature (more mature than many, many grown-ups I know)? Start learning to be "quick to hear, slow to speak, slow to anger" (James 1:19 ESV). Not only will you be more mature, you will find and keep truer friends and have better relationships with them and your family.

Watching what you say
can save you a lot of trouble.
PROVERBS 21:23 CEV

A kind answer soothes angry feelings, but harsh words
stir them up. Words of wisdom come from the wise,
but fools speak foolishness. The Lord sees everything,
whether good or bad. Kind words are good medicine,
but deceitful words can really hurt.

PROVERBS 15:1–4 CEV

Sharp words cut like a sword,
but words of wisdom heal.

PROVERBS 12:18 CEV

Keep your tongue from speaking
evil and your lips from telling lies!

PSALM 34:13 NLT

"Do you really love life? Do you want to be happy?
Then stop saying cruel things and quit telling lies."

1 PETER 3:10 CEV

The tongue can bring death or life; those who
love to talk will reap the consequences.

PROVERBS 18:21 NLT

"The food that you put into your mouth doesn't make you
unclean and unfit to worship God. The bad words that
come out of your mouth are what make you unclean."

MATTHEW 15:11 CEV

Your written words matter, too, whether it's in your diary or journal, or on e-mails, texts, and social media sites like Facebook and Twitter. Don't forget all these scriptures when you're communicating in these ways, being especially careful because when your words are written down and maybe sent over the Internet, they're very easy for someone to copy and potentially use against you.

It's very smart to follow the Bible's advice:

Don't use foul or abusive language. Let everything you say be good and helpful, so that your words will be an encouragement to those who hear them.
EPHESIANS 4:29 NLT

It's a huge challenge to watch carefully over our words. You will make mistakes at times, but keep this as your prayer:

Take control of what I say,
O LORD, and guard my lips.
PSALM 141:3 NLT

Jesus will always be so happy to help you!

It All Matters to Jesus

❋ Everything you say, speak, or write matters to Jesus.

❋ What you say to your parents matters to Jesus.

❋ What you say to your siblings matters to Jesus.

❋ What you say to your friends matters to Jesus.

❋ What you say to your teachers and youth leaders matters to Jesus.

❋ What you say on social media matters to Jesus.

❋ What you write in your blog or journal matters to Jesus.

❋ Being quick to listen, slow to speak, and slow to become angry matters to Jesus.

❋ Being able to control your words matters to Jesus.

❋ Being encouraging, kind, and helpful with your words matters to Jesus.

What Comes Out—Your Actions

Have you ever had classmates or known people at Sunday school who act sugary sweet and obedient when the teacher is watching, and as soon as the teacher turns around, they're mean or they're trying to cheat off your paper or they're breaking all the rules? They're sort of like that creepy old story of Dr. Jekyll and Mr. Hyde. It's so frustrating!

And, unfortunately, there are all sorts of religious leaders and grown-ups in our world today who say one thing and do another—they pretend to love and follow Jesus and the Bible, but if someone looks closer into how they live their lives. . .things start looking weird. . . things just don't add up.

People who continuously act like this are called hypocrites, and it matters a lot to Jesus that we do not act like hypocrites. It matters to Jesus that our "what comes out" matches our "what goes in" about Him. How we act as Christians should line up with what we say about our faith in Jesus, and what we say about Him should match what His Word says is true about Him.

There are a lot of strong verses in the Bible that talk about hypocrites:

Not everyone who calls me their Lord will get into the kingdom of heaven. Only the ones who obey my Father in heaven will get in. On the day of judgment many will call me their Lord. They will say, "We preached in your name, and in your name we forced out demons and worked many miracles." But I will tell them, "I will have nothing to do with you! Get out of my sight, you evil people!"

MATTHEW 7:21-23 CEV

"You hypocrites! Isaiah was right when he prophesied about you, for he wrote, 'These people honor me with their lips, but their hearts are far from me. Their worship is a farce, for they teach man-made ideas as commands from God.'"

MATTHEW 15:7-9 NLT

Whoever says "I know him" but does not keep his commandments is a liar, and the truth is not in him.

1 JOHN 2:4 ESV

Whoever says he is in the light and hates his brother is still in darkness.

1 JOHN 2:9 ESV

My friends, what good is it to say you have faith, when you don't do anything to show that you really do have faith? Can that kind of faith save you? If you know someone who doesn't have any clothes or food, you shouldn't just say, "I hope all goes well for you. I hope you will be warm and have plenty to eat." What good is it to say this, unless you do something to help? Faith that doesn't lead us to do good deeds is all alone and dead! Suppose someone disagrees and says, "It is possible to have faith without doing kind deeds." I would answer, "Prove that you have faith without doing kind deeds, and I will prove that I have faith by doing them." You surely believe there is only one God. That's fine. Even demons believe this, and it makes them shake with fear.

JAMES 2:14–19 CEV

If we say we have fellowship with him while we walk in darkness, we lie and do not practice the truth.

1 JOHN 1:6 ESV

I'm sure you've heard the old saying that "actions speak louder than words." It's absolutely true. Be careful that the way you live your life and the way you treat others matches up with what you say about loving Jesus. Mostly, if you say you love Jesus, your actions will overflow with obedience to His Word and boundless love for others. Being a "doer of the Word" matters *so much* to Jesus.

But be doers of the word, and not hearers only, deceiving yourselves. For if anyone is a hearer of the word and not a doer, he is like a man who looks intently at his natural face in a mirror. For he looks at himself and goes away and at once forgets what he was like. But the one who looks into the perfect law, the law of liberty, and perseveres, being no hearer who forgets but a doer who acts, he will be blessed in his doing.
JAMES 1:22–25 ESV

It All Matters to Jesus

❀ Everything you do matters to Jesus.

❀ *Not* being a hypocrite matters to Jesus.

❀ Matching what you do to what you say matters to Jesus.

❀ Not just saying but *showing* that you are a Christian matters to Jesus.

❀ Obeying God and His Word matters to Jesus.

❀ Proving your faith by your good deeds matters to Jesus.

❀ Loving others matters to Jesus.

❀ Being doers, not just hearers, of the Word matters to Jesus.

Color with Love

Do you still like to color? I do! I especially love a brand-new box of crayons or markers. And there are so many fun kinds these days. Twistable crayons, glittery crayons, watercolor-paint crayons. . .so many supercool options to create a beautiful work of art.

Imagine that you could wake up every morning and see outlined coloring-book pages of your day, kind of like a black-and-white comic strip. Now imagine picking out the love-colored crayon (whatever color that looks like to you!) and shading in each picture. That's what Jesus wants us to do, to color everything we do, every day we have on this earth with love. Love matters to Him so much, and by loving others, we share His love. He said in John 13:34–35 (ESV), "A new commandment I give to you, that you love one another: just as I have loved you, you also are to love one another. By this all people will know that you are my disciples, if you have love for one another."

Here are just a handful of ways you can color your day with love:

✳ When you get a good grade on a test, it's great to be happy, but you can also be humble and not brag about it or flaunt it in any of your classmates' faces, especially some who might not have done well.

Let all that you do be done in love.
1 Corinthians 16:14 esv

✳ When your sibling picks a fight with you, either do your best to work it out and be a peacemaker or walk away until you can get a parent or other grown-up to help.

"Put on then, as God's chosen ones, holy and beloved, compassionate hearts, kindness, humility, meekness, and patience, bearing with one another and, if one has a complaint against another, forgiving each other; as the Lord has forgiven you, so you also must forgive. And above all these put on love, which binds everything together in perfect harmony."
Colossians 3:12-14 esv

✽ When it's unfair that Mom promised to take you to the mall, but the car broke down, offer her love and understanding that you can reschedule for another time.

Above all, love each other deeply,
because love covers over a multitude of sins.
1 PETER 4:8 NIV

✽ When you're so frustrated that Dad promised to shoot hoops with you but he had to work late three nights in a row at a very stressful job, instead of being upset find a way to encourage him.

Always be humble and gentle. Patiently put
up with each other and love each other.
EPHESIANS 4:2 CEV

✽ When you see Mom and Dad are extra tired, help make supper, set the table, and look for little chores that need done without being asked.

Dear children, let us not love with words
or speech but with actions and in truth.
1 JOHN 3:18 NIV

✽ When you are blessed with a special treat, share it with a friend or sibling.

✳ When you see a friend in Sunday school who feels shy and left out, invite that person into your circle of friends.

One of the teachers of religious law was standing there listening to the debate. He realized that Jesus had answered well, so he asked, "Of all the commandments, which is the most important?" Jesus replied, "The most important commandment is this: 'Listen, O Israel! The LORD our God is the one and only LORD. And you must love the LORD your God with all your heart, all your soul, all your mind, and all your strength.' The second is equally important: 'Love your neighbor as yourself.' No other commandment is greater than these."

MARK 12:28-31 NLT

✳ When a classmate is acting mean to you, share your dessert with her at lunchtime.

"Love your enemies! Do good to them. Lend to them without expecting to be repaid. Then your reward from heaven will be very great, and you will truly be acting as children of the Most High, for he is kind to those who are unthankful and wicked. You must be compassionate, just as your Father is compassionate."

LUKE 6:35-36 NLT

Some of the most famous love verses of the Bible are found in 1 Corinthians 13. They describe what true love looks like, the way we should strive to love everyone around us all the time:

What if I could speak all languages of humans and of angels? If I did not love others, I would be nothing more than a noisy gong or a clanging cymbal. What if I could prophesy and understand all secrets and all knowledge? And what if I had faith that moved mountains? I would be nothing, unless I loved others. What if I gave away all that I owned and let myself be burned alive? I would gain nothing, unless I loved others. Love is kind and patient, never jealous, boastful, proud, or rude. Love isn't selfish or quick tempered. It doesn't keep a record of wrongs that others do. Love rejoices in the truth, but not in evil. Love is always supportive, loyal, hopeful, and trusting. Love never fails!

1 CORINTHIANS 13:1–8 CEV

You might wonder, *If I'm doing all these loving things, what good is it for me? Who's going to be showing love for me?* You will be amazed at the return on your investment. Loving others makes you incredibly lovable. Not only will other people see your love and want to return it, but God especially sees and He will bless you and fill your heart to bursting with satisfaction and joy. Loving is what God made us for!

My dear friends, we must love each other. Love comes from God, and when we love each other, it shows that we have been given new life. We are now God's children, and we know him. God is love, and anyone who doesn't love others has never known him. God showed his love for us when he sent his only Son into the world to give us life. Real love isn't our love for God, but his love for us. God sent his Son to be the sacrifice by which our sins are forgiven. Dear friends, since God loved us this much, we must love each other. No one has ever seen God. But if we love each other, God lives in us, and his love is truly in our hearts.

1 JOHN 4:7–12 CEV

It All Matters to Jesus

❀ Loving your parents matters to Jesus.

❀ Loving your siblings matters to Jesus.

❀ Loving your friends matters to Jesus.

❀ Loving your enemies matters to Jesus.

❀ Letting love color everything you do matters to Jesus.

The Truth, the Whole Truth, and Nothing but the Truth

Think about a time when a friend lied to you. Did you like it? Did it make it hard to trust her again?

Now think about a time when you lied to your parents and were caught. What were the consequences? Was it worth it?

Here is just a little of what the Bible says about lying:

Do not tell lies about others.
EXODUS 20:16 CEV

If you do the right thing, honesty will be your guide. But if you are crooked, you will be trapped by your own dishonesty.
PROVERBS 11:3 CEV

The LORD detests lying lips, but he delights in those who tell the truth.
PROVERBS 12:22 NLT

A false witness will not go unpunished, and a liar will be destroyed.
PROVERBS 19:9 NLT

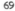

Unfortunately, lying is so common these days. It's hard to find the truth sometimes, so it's incredibly important that those of us who love and follow Jesus stand strong in the truth—about everything!

It might seem like "little white lies" and bending the truth when we need to are no big deal, but they are! Because if you start out willing to lie about little things, then at some point you're likely willing to lie about big things.

People who aren't totally committed to living honest lives end up being people who can't really be trusted with much of anything.

Do you want to be a person whom others can trust? Do you want your parents and teachers and leaders at church to give you important tasks and responsibilities, knowing that you'll follow through on them? Do you want to have friends who feel safe telling you anything at all because they know you won't blab it around where it doesn't need to be told? Or do you want to be the girl whom grown-ups know they have to keep a constant eye on and have to question everything she's doing? Or the one that other girls are afraid to talk to because she spreads so much gossip?

*"If you are faithful in little things, you will be faithful
in large ones. But if you are dishonest in little things,
you won't be honest with greater responsibilities.
And if you are untrustworthy about worldly wealth,
who will trust you with the true riches of heaven?
And if you are not faithful with other people's things,
why should you be trusted with things of your own?"*
LUKE 16:10–12 NLT

If you don't want to be *that* girl who can't be trusted
(who ends up being that grown-up with all kinds of
problems), then start now being honest in Every. Single.
Thing. You. Do.

Tell the truth, even if there are consequences.
(Believe me, the consequences won't be as bad if you're
honest about the problem.) Have integrity. Proverbs 10:9
(ESV) says, "Whoever walks in integrity walks securely,
but he who makes his ways crooked will be found out."
And Proverbs 19:1 (ESV) says, "Better is a poor person
who walks in his integrity than one who is crooked in
speech and is a fool."

Follow through when you make a commitment. If there are circumstances beyond your control that make it impossible to keep a commitment, then give a heads-up to whomever you're reporting to. Be consistent about doing what you say you will do. You've heard guys say, "I'm a man of my word." Well, you should strive to be a girl of your word—who will end up becoming an awesome woman of your word!

And never forget why we tell the truth and what we base our truth on—Jesus Himself.

Jesus answered, "I am the way and the truth and the life. No one comes to the Father except through me."
JOHN 14:6 NIV

If you are leading an honest life, always telling the truth, you will help others come to know Jesus as the Way, the Truth, and the Life.

If you have messed up and lied, then go and make it right with God, knowing that "if we confess our sins, he is faithful and just and will forgive us our sins and purify us from all unrighteousness" (1 John 1:9 NIV).

It All Matters to Jesus

❋ Telling the truth matters to Jesus.

❋ Having integrity matters to Jesus.

❋ Keeping commitments matters to Jesus.

❋ Being able to be trusted with a little matters to Jesus.

❋ Being able to be trusted with a lot matters to Jesus.

Heartbreak

What's the saddest thing that you've ever experienced? Has a close friend moved away? Have your parents gotten divorced? Has a favorite pet died? Have you lost a loved one to cancer or a car accident? Maybe you're blessed that none of these have happened to you, but you've watched and tried to comfort a friend or family member who has gone through them. Because of sin, our broken world is so full of hurt and sadness that it just seems completely overwhelming at times.

Among other terrible hurts, I've held my favorite pet in my arms as they gave him the shot to put him to sleep—and I was completely heartbroken. I held my grandpa's hand and heard him struggle for every breath as he lay dying of cancer—and I was completely heartbroken.

I'm sure you've been heartbroken in some way before, too.

The bright spot in our saddest circumstances is this promise from the Bible: "The LORD is close to the brokenhearted; he rescues those whose spirits are crushed" (Psalm 34:18 NLT).

When your heart is breaking, don't ever forget that He hasn't left you. He has promised, "Never will I leave you; never will I forsake you" (Hebrews 13:5 NIV). Maybe you don't feel like it. Maybe you feel like He's forgotten you or you can't understand how or why awful things happen to good people. But in those moments, you have a choice to turn away from God because you're mad at Him, or you can choose to draw closer to Him and trust Him despite your hurt—and let Him comfort you and help you through the dark, sad days. Little by little they *will* get better. His Word says, "Come close to God, and God will come close to you" (James 4:8 NLT). And "The LORD is near to all who call on him, to all who call on him in truth" (Psalm 145:18 ESV).

When life is at its worst, the worst thing you can do is run from God. If you stick it out and stay close to Him, He will carry you through it.

And remember that because Jesus rose from the grave, He defeated sin and death, and we have awesome hope and confidence that one day all the hurt in this world will end and we will never, ever be sad again. These verses from 1 Peter are so encouraging:

Praise God, the Father of our Lord Jesus Christ. God is so good, and by raising Jesus from death, he has given us new life and a hope that lives on. God has something stored up for you in heaven, where it will never decay or be ruined or disappear. You have faith in God, whose power will protect you until the last day. Then he will save you, just as he has always planned to do. On that day you will be glad, even if you have to go through many hard trials for a while. Your faith will be like gold that has been tested in a fire. And these trials will prove that your faith is worth much more than gold that can be destroyed. They will show that you will be given praise and honor and glory when Jesus Christ returns.
1 PETER 1:3–7 CEV

No matter how sad you are or how bad life hurts you, don't ever give up! We "live by faith, not by what we see" (2 Corinthians 5:7 CEV), and our faith is in a living Savior and in a place where all things will be made right someday—heaven, where "God will make his home among his people. He will wipe all tears from their eyes, and there will be no more death, suffering, crying, or pain" (Revelation 21:3–4 CEV).

We can rejoice, too, when we run into problems and trials, for we know that they help us develop endurance. And endurance develops strength of character, and character strengthens our confident hope of salvation. And this hope will not lead to disappointment. For we know how dearly God loves us, because he has given us the Holy Spirit to fill our hearts with his love.
ROMANS 5:3–5 NLT

It All Matters to Jesus

❀ All your hurts matter to Jesus.

❀ If a friend breaks your heart, it matters to Jesus.

❀ If you're hurting over your parents' divorce, it matters to Jesus.

❀ If a loved one dies, it matters to Jesus.

❀ If you have to put a favorite pet to sleep, it matters to Jesus.

❀ Drawing close to Him when you are hurting matters to Jesus.

❀ Trusting Him when you are hurting matters to Jesus.

❀ Not giving up when you are hurting matters to Jesus.

In the Mirror

How much time do you spend in front of the mirror? Are you a girl who likes to take awhile getting your hair just right, or would you rather throw it in a ponytail and be done? Do you like pretty jewelry and accessories to match your outfits, or could you not care less about that kind of stuff? Do you like skirts and dresses or jeans and T-shirts? Or maybe it just depends on your mood?

No matter if you wear sparkly barrettes and headbands that perfectly coordinate with your clothes every day or if you use the same simple ponytail holder with any outfit because it always matches, Jesus cares about looks—but not in the way the world cares. Our culture likes to make us think we have to have the latest fashions, huge bright eyes, and perfect hair to be beautiful. But Jesus cares what your heart looks like, and if your heart is beautiful, then your beauty shines brighter than any model on any magazine cover. The Bible says, "People judge by outward appearance, but the LORD looks at the heart" (1 Samuel 16:7 NLT).

And what's He looking for in your heart?

First off, it matters if your heart has had a Jesus makeover, meaning you believe in Him and have asked Him to be your Savior and Lord over your life. It's incredible to think that Jesus died and became the sacrifice for our sin so that God, who is so good and holy, can look at us and not see our ugly sin; but He sees us as righteous, just like it says in 1 Corinthians 1:30 (NLT): "Christ made us right with God; he made us pure and holy, and he freed us from sin." And in 2 Corinthians 5:21 (NLT): "For God made Christ, who never sinned, to be the offering for our sin, so that we could be made right with God through Christ."

I hope you are incredibly thankful for that! I hope it gives you goose bumps or makes you want to cry happy tears!

It seems like you could just stop there, doesn't it? If Jesus already did the work of forgiving your sins and you accept that and God sees you as righteous, then it's all good, everything is beautiful, and you can live your life any way you want because everything is forgiven. But here's the deal: a *true* relationship with Jesus is active, and it never stops seeking God and His will for your life. God made you for a purpose! He sees you as so beautiful when you are doing the things He planned for you to do.

Ephesians 2:10 (NIV) says, "For we are God's handiwork, created in Christ Jesus to do good works, which God prepared in advance for us to do."

Don't ever stop asking God what those good works are that He has for you to do, and don't ever stop praying and reading His Word to find out.

Here are a couple more verses on God's idea of beautiful—which should be our idea of beautiful, too:

*Don't be concerned about the outward beauty of fancy
hairstyles, expensive jewelry, or beautiful clothes.
You should clothe yourselves instead with the beauty
that comes from within, the unfading beauty of a gentle
and quiet spirit, which is so precious to God.*

1 PETER 3:3-4 NLT

*Charm can be deceiving, and beauty fades away, but a
woman who honors the LORD deserves to be praised. Show
her respect—praise her in public for what she has done.*

PROVERBS 31:30-31 CEV

The bottom line is, true beauty comes from within,
from a spirit that is gentle and quietly seeking God and
honoring Him in every area of life. If you are doing those
things, you can't help but shine the stunning light of
Jesus and real beauty to everyone around you.

What about physical fitness and perfectly tan and toned bodies? Our culture sure puts a lot of emphasis on how amazing those things are. Being healthy certainly is great, and God wants us to take good care of our bodies. He even says that our bodies are a temple: "Do you not know that your bodies are temples of the Holy Spirit, who is in you, whom you have received from God? You are not your own; you were bought at a price. Therefore honor God with your bodies" (1 Corinthians 6:19-20 NIV).

But we should never be obsessed with physical fitness, as so many in our world are today. It seems like too many people are one extreme or the other—either they have no desire to truly care for their bodies or they are consumed with making sure they eat exactly the right foods and exercise in exactly the right way so that every muscle is in exactly the right condition. Neither of those is right. What's right is a healthy balance, and this verse sums it up perfectly:

For physical training is of some value, but godliness has value for all things, holding promise for both the present life and the life to come.
1 TIMOTHY 4:8 NIV

Keeping our bodies healthy matters for this life so that we can actually do the good works God has planned for us to do, but eventually these earthly bodies of ours will wear out. So godly fitness—keeping our spirits and minds and hearts healthy by training them in God's Word and with prayer and with serving others and going to church—is what has value forever in heaven.

So, does Jesus care that you're upset when you're having a hideous hair day? Or if you have a ginormous bruise on your face from playing softball and it's picture day at school? Absolutely! He cares in that He loves you and wants to help you through those hard things, but nothing like that ever means you are less beautiful to Him. And when you are beautiful to the Creator God of the universe, who is the King of all kings, then think about this—does it really matter at all who else thinks you are beautiful or not? You are to God, and that is always enough!

It All Matters to Jesus

❄ Being beautiful on the inside matters to Jesus.

❄ It's the heart, not the outward looks, that matters most to Jesus.

❄ Having a Jesus makeover, letting Him get rid of your ugly sin, matters to Jesus.

❄ Physical fitness matters to Jesus, but godly fitness matters more.

❄ Gentle and quiet spirits matter to Jesus.

❄ Honoring the Lord matters to Jesus.

Gimme, Gimme, Gimme!

It's funny how if you watch commercials on TV or look at ads online or catalogs from the mail, you start thinking you just have to have the latest toys, games, shoes, and clothes. Everything looks so cool, doesn't it? It kinda makes you want to say, "Gimme, gimme, gimme!!" Have you been begging your parents for anything lately? Is there a particular gift you're hoping for on your birthday or Christmas?

It's not bad to want some nice things, and giving us good gifts matters to Jesus. He gave us the best gift ever, after all—Himself, as the Savior of our sins— and He's preparing a ginormous gift of a forever home in heaven with Him.

Here is some of what the Bible has to say about God's best gift to us:

You were saved by faith in God, who treats us much better than we deserve. This is God's gift to you, and not anything you have done on your own. It isn't something you have earned, so there is nothing you can brag about.
EPHESIANS 2:8-9 CEV

For all have sinned and fall short of the glory of God,
and are justified by his grace as a gift,
through the redemption that is in Christ Jesus.
ROMANS 3:23-24 ESV

Thank God for his gift that is too wonderful for words!
2 CORINTHIANS 9:15 CEV

On top of the best gift of all, God is giving us gifts along the way, too, in our daily lives. Look at these verses:

"You parents—if your children ask for a loaf of bread, do you give them a stone instead? Or if they ask for a fish, do you give them a snake? Of course not! So if you sinful people know how to give good gifts to your children, how much more will your heavenly Father give good gifts to those who ask him."
MATTHEW 7:9-11 NLT

Whatever is good and perfect is a gift coming down to us from God our Father, who created all the lights in the heavens. He never changes or casts a shifting shadow.
JAMES 1:17 NLT

Sometimes you receive a gift that you don't really want. Do you like getting plain white socks for Christmas? Or toothpaste in your stocking? Those aren't that fun. But they *are* things that you need.

It's important to learn when you are very young the difference between needs and wants. And it's important to be thankful for receiving the things that you need and realizing that sometimes getting the things you want is just an awesome added bonus!

We don't need the latest fashions, but we do need warm clothes, and God promises to provide them:

"Look at the lilies and how they grow. They don't work or make their clothing, yet Solomon in all his glory was not dressed as beautifully as they are. And if God cares so wonderfully for flowers that are here today and thrown into the fire tomorrow, he will certainly care for you."
LUKE 12:27-28 NLT

We don't need gourmet meals or to eat at restaurants all the time, but we do need healthy foods, and God will make sure we have them:

"And don't be concerned about what to eat and what to drink. Don't worry about such things. These things dominate the thoughts of unbelievers all over the world, but your Father already knows your needs."
LUKE 12:29-30 NLT

When Jesus teaches us to pray in the Bible, He says, "Give us this day our daily bread" (Matthew 6:11 NKJV). He doesn't add this to the prayer: "And I need doughnuts for tomorrow and bagels and cream cheese, and milk to go with that, and then maybe a cookie. And what are we going to eat the day after that?" No. He says *daily bread*, meaning simply what we need to keep us going each day, without worrying about the next day or the day after that.

We need to focus on how rich we are, without *stuff*. As Christians we are called to "seek the Kingdom of God above all else, and live righteously, and he will give you everything you need" (Matthew 6:33 NLT). That means our purpose should not be to pile up stuff that we can't take with us when we die, but to focus on God and obeying Him and letting Him provide everything we need.

The Bible also says to "take delight in the LORD, and he will give you the desires of your heart" (Psalm 37:4 NIV). Does that mean that as long as you are happy with God, then He will get you those new shoes you're drooling over, or that new iPod or bike or game or whatever? Sometimes maybe, just as an added bonus, but mostly it means when your happiness is focused on God, He will be changing your heart so that you constantly find your joy and satisfy your desires by just knowing and serving and loving Him.

It All Matters to Jesus

❀ Your wants matter to Jesus.

❀ Your needs matter more to Jesus.

❀ Learning the difference between wants and needs matters to Jesus.

❀ Realizing that all good gifts come from God matters to Jesus.

❀ Being thankful for gifts (even socks and toothpaste!) matters to Jesus.

❀ Seeking God first, before *stuff*, matters to Jesus.

❀ Finding your happiness in Him rather than stuff matters to Jesus.

From Pet Peeves to Seeing Red

Do you have a pet peeve—something common that bothers you? Like someone squeezing the toothpaste tube from the middle rather than the bottom. Toilet paper under instead of over, or the opposite. People cutting in line. When someone tries to talk to you when you're reading. When your mom asks you to hurry up and get ready to go RIGHT! NOW! but then you wait in the car for what seems like forever while *she* finishes getting ready.

Ugh! Those things can make you irritated, but what makes you *really angry*? Or as some people describe it, what makes you see red? (Picture those funny characters on old cartoons, with their faces colored crimson and steam coming from their ears!) Do your friends ever cause drama over nothing? Do your parents punish you too quickly before listening to your side sometimes? Have you been lied to? Gossiped about? Maybe even things much worse than this. . .

But the Bible tells us to be very careful with anger:

Control your temper,
for anger labels you a fool.
ECCLESIASTES 7:9 NLT

Fools vent their anger,
but the wise quietly hold it back.
PROVERBS 29:11 NLT

A kind answer soothes angry feelings,
but harsh words stir them up.
PROVERBS 15:1 CEV

Good sense makes one slow to anger,
and it is his glory to overlook an offense.
PROVERBS 19:11 ESV

The LORD is merciful and gracious, slow to
anger and abounding in steadfast love.
PSALM 103:8 ESV

Stop being bitter and angry and mad at others.
Don't yell at one another or curse each other or ever be
rude. Instead, be kind and merciful, and forgive others,
just as God forgave you because of Christ.
EPHESIANS 4:31-32 CEV

You must quit being angry, hateful, and evil. You must
no longer say insulting or cruel things about others.
COLOSSIANS 3:8 CEV

It's a seriously messed-up world that we live in. Unfortunately, there are lots of things that are going to make you angry in your life. *Lots* of things. It is okay, even good, to be angry sometimes. The Bible actually *says* to be angry:

> *Be angry, and do not sin; ponder in your own hearts on your beds, and be silent. Offer right sacrifices, and put your trust in the LORD.*
> PSALM 4:4–5 ESV

> *Be angry and do not sin; do not let the sun go down on your anger, and give no opportunity to the devil.*
> EPHESIANS 4:26–27 ESV

But it's extremely important for you to control how quickly you become angry and how you react in your anger:

> *Be patient and trust the LORD. Don't let it bother you when all goes well for those who do sinful things. Don't be angry or furious. Anger can lead to sin.*
> PSALM 37:7–8 CEV

> *Understand this, my dear brothers and sisters: You must all be quick to listen, slow to speak, and slow to get angry. Human anger does not produce the righteousness God desires.*
> JAMES 1:19–20 NLT

Basically, we should not dive headfirst into the deep end of anger when something goes wrong. And when we are angry, we cannot use that as an excuse to sin. Did you notice that both of those verses that said "be angry" also said "do not sin"?

Even when seriously unfair and horrible stuff has been done to us, we are not supposed to retaliate or "get even." The Bible says:

Dear friends, don't try to get even. Let God take revenge. In the Scriptures the Lord says, "I am the one to take revenge and pay them back." The Scriptures also say, "If your enemies are hungry, give them something to eat. And if they are thirsty, give them something to drink. This will be the same as piling burning coals on their heads." Don't let evil defeat you, but defeat evil with good.
ROMANS 12:19-21 CEV

We have to control ourselves and do our very best not to sin. In other words, if your little sister pours a bottle of bubbles all over the art project you just spent twelve hours on, it's not wrong of you to feel angry. That would totally stink! But it's not okay to be so angry that you go break her favorite toy to get even.

If a classmate cheats off your paper and gets you both in trouble, it's okay to be mad. It's not okay to snatch her homework and tear it up the next day. When you feel the emotion of anger, you need to slow it down, not let it overcome you. Count to ten or even one hundred, run to your bedroom and cry into your pillow, whatever calming action helps you take a little time-out to get your feelings under control. Most of all, ask God to help you deal with it in the right way. Ask Him to calm you down and give you wisdom on how to get help and make things right.

And admit it, sometimes you get really angry over stuff that truly is not a big deal. We all do. When we're feeling tired, impatient, or stressed out, sometimes the things that maybe should be a little pet peeve make us freak and lash out with really angry words and/or actions. When that happens, you need to make it right. You need to apologize and ask forgiveness from the person you acted out on, and you need to take it to God for His forgiveness and for His help to deal with it better in the future. It's truly an ongoing challenge, but one that Jesus will always help you with—because how you deal with anger matters so much to Him.

It All Matters to Jesus

❀ Being slow to get angry matters to Jesus.

❀ When you do feel angry, controlling it matters to Jesus.

❀ Letting God do the "getting even" matters to Jesus.

❀ Apologizing when you've acted in anger matters to Jesus.

❀ Choosing kind words instead of angry words matters to Jesus.

Flying Monkeys and Other Fears

Do you like the classic movie *The Wizard of Oz*? I love it, but when I was little, I was scared of the Wicked Witch of the West—and I was completely *terrified* of her flying monkeys! They were so creepy! I vividly remember hiding behind the couch when they came on the screen and having a couple of nightmares about them. Now I can look back and laugh about that, but I still have fears. Everyone does, no matter what age you are. Our fears just change a bit with each year we grow older and with each new life experience we have.

I don't want to write a list of things you might be scared of, in case I mention one you haven't thought of and it becomes a new fear for you. That wouldn't be very nice of me! I'm sure it's not hard for you to think of things that make you scared, the things that keep you awake at night or keep you from doing the things you'd like to do. But you just need to know that God is bigger than every single one of your fears, and He wants to take them from you and give you peace about them.

There are so many encouraging scriptures that you can read to help you with your fears. The best thing you can do to conquer your fears is to memorize verses to fight them, and when you feel the fear creeping up on you, keep saying the verse over and over and let God's power and peace conquer that fear!

Fear not, for I am with you; be not dismayed, for I am your God; I will strengthen you, I will help you, I will uphold you with my righteous right hand.
ISAIAH 41:10 ESV

Don't worry about anything; instead, pray about everything. Tell God what you need, and thank him for all he has done. Then you will experience God's peace, which exceeds anything we can understand. His peace will guard your hearts and minds as you live in Christ Jesus.
PHILIPPIANS 4:6–7 NLT

When I am afraid, I put my trust in you.
PSALM 56:3 ESV

For God gave us a spirit not of fear
but of power and love and self-control.
2 TIMOTHY 1:7 ESV

"Be strong and courageous. Do not fear or be in dread
of them, for it is the LORD your God who goes with you.
He will not leave you or forsake you."
DEUTERONOMY 31:6 ESV

I asked the LORD for help, and he
saved me from all my fears.
PSALM 34:4 CEV

"Have I not commanded you? Be strong and courageous.
Do not be afraid; do not be discouraged, for the LORD
your God will be with you wherever you go."
JOSHUA 1:9 NIV

Say to those with fearful hearts, "Be strong,
and do not fear, for your God is coming to
destroy your enemies. He is coming to save you."
ISAIAH 35:4 NLT

"I am leaving you with a gift—peace of mind and heart.
And the peace I give is a gift the world cannot give.
So don't be troubled or afraid."
JOHN 14:27 NLT

No, in all these things we are more than conquerors through him who loved us. For I am convinced that neither death nor life, neither angels nor demons, neither the present nor the future, nor any powers, neither height nor depth, nor anything else in all creation, will be able to separate us from the love of God that is in Christ Jesus our Lord.

ROMANS 8:37-39 NIV

Now, who will want to harm you if you are eager to do good? But even if you suffer for doing what is right, God will reward you for it. So don't worry or be afraid of their threats. Instead, you must worship Christ as Lord of your life.

1 PETER 3:13-15 NLT

*Even though I walk through the valley of the shadow
of death, I will fear no evil, for you are with me;
your rod and your staff, they comfort me.*

PSALM 23:4 ESV

*The LORD is my light and my salvation—
whom shall I fear? The LORD is the stronghold
of my life—of whom shall I be afraid?*

PSALM 27:1 NIV

*The LORD is on my side; I will not fear.
What can man do to me?*

PSALM 118:6 ESV

*God is our refuge and strength, always ready to
help in times of trouble. So we will not fear when
earthquakes come and the mountains crumble
into the sea. Let the oceans roar and foam.
Let the mountains tremble as the waters surge!*

PSALM 46:1-3 NLT

*My enemies chase me all day. Many of them are pursuing
and attacking me, but even when I am afraid, I keep
on trusting you. I praise your promises! I trust you
and am not afraid. No one can harm me.*

PSALM 56:1-4 CEV

It All Matters to Jesus

❋ Your big fears matter to Jesus.

❋ Your little fears matter to Jesus.

❋ Praying when you are afraid matters to Jesus.

❋ Trusting in God when you are afraid matters to Jesus.

❋ Memorizing scripture to fight fear matters to Jesus.

❋ Knowing that God is on your side matters to Jesus.

❋ Helping others who are afraid matters to Jesus.

Live and Learn

It's amazing and awesome how many options there are these days for different ways of doing school. Public schools, private schools, charter schools, homeschool, e-schools, just to name a few. There's even something called unschooling! There are so many different ways for any type of learner to get a good education and fit the type of lifestyle that you and your family have.

So, how do you do school? Are you happy with it, or do you wish you were able to do something different? Do you enjoy school or just kind of suffer through it? Are you eager to learn and work hard, or do all the assignments and studying seem like such a drag? Do you like to learn in traditional ways or do you need to do things in a totally unique way?

There are positives and negatives about each different kind of school. There are good days and bad with any kind. There are some assignments and subjects we have to force ourselves to get through and others that we love to do! Whether you're mostly happy with school or not, your attitude toward it matters to Jesus.

The Bible says, "Whatever you do, work at it with all your heart, as working for the Lord" (Colossians 3:23 NIV). *Whatever you do*, yes even the math assignments that make you crazy, or the daily reading assignments that take forever, or the science fair project that seems so overwhelming. And the parts that you love or are supereasy for you, do those with your whole heart, too! God wants you to give your very best effort to doing your work well. Think of turning in each assignment not just to your teacher, but to the God of the universe, the Creator of all learning, who loves you more than anyone else does! When you do your best with a good attitude, you show the excellence He has created you for, which brings Him praise and honor and ends up showing His light and love to those around you.

Here is some of what the Bible has to say about learning:

Do you see someone skilled in their work?
They will serve before kings; they will
not serve before officials of low rank.

PROVERBS 22:29 NIV

Commit yourself to instruction;
listen carefully to words of knowledge.

PROVERBS 23:12 NLT

Commit your work to the LORD,
and your plans will be established.

PROVERBS 16:3 ESV

Intelligent people are always ready to learn.
Their ears are open for knowledge.

PROVERBS 18:15 NLT

If you have good sense, you will learn all you can,
but foolish talk will soon destroy you.

PROVERBS 10:14 CEV

If you have good sense, instruction will help you
to have even better sense. And if you live right,
education will help you to know even more.

PROVERBS 9:9 CEV

Better and more important than any book knowledge or high test scores or college degrees, though, is this command:

> *Respect and obey the LORD!*
> *This is the beginning of wisdom. To have*
> *understanding, you must know the Holy God.*
> PROVERBS 9:10 CEV

Respecting and obeying the Lord, or fearing Him as some versions of this verse put it, is the starting point for any real wisdom. People could grow up learning in the very best schools, getting the highest grades and test scores and the best degree in college. They could have all the worldly smarts you can think of, but if they don't know and obey and respect God, then all that is for nothing in the end, and they don't have true wisdom.

As you're living and learning and growing up, you also need to be very careful to compare every new thing you learn to God's Word. Many people in the world will try to tell you the Bible is not true and that believing in Jesus and living a Christian life is silly. They'll have lots of convincing-sounding evidence to back up their talk, too. But when you are tested in that way, remember the following verses and keep yourself closely walking with God, ask Christian grown-ups to help you with the questions you have, stay involved in a Bible-teaching church, and ask God to show you more and more of His truth.

Above all, you must realize that no prophecy in Scripture ever came from the prophet's own understanding, or from human initiative. No, those prophets were moved by the Holy Spirit, and they spoke from God.

2 PETER 1:20-21 NLT

And we also thank God continually because, when you received the word of God, which you heard from us, you accepted it not as a human word, but as it actually is, the word of God, which is indeed at work in you who believe.

1 Thessalonians 2:13 niv

For the word of God is living and active, sharper than any two-edged sword, piercing to the division of soul and of spirit, of joints and of marrow, and discerning the thoughts and intentions of the heart.

Hebrews 4:12 esv

Just as you accepted Christ Jesus as your Lord, you must continue to follow him. Let your roots grow down into him, and let your lives be built on him. Then your faith will grow strong in the truth you were taught, and you will overflow with thankfulness. Don't let anyone capture you with empty philosophies and high-sounding nonsense that come from human thinking and from the spiritual powers of this world, rather than from Christ.

Colossians 2:6–8 nlt

It All Matters to Jesus

❋ Your education matters to Jesus.

❋ Doing your best on your schoolwork matters to Jesus.

❋ Comparing everything you learn to the Bible matters to Jesus.

❋ Learning at a Bible-teaching church matters to Jesus.

❋ Your good days at school matter to Jesus.

❋ Your bad days at school matter to Jesus.

❋ Fearing God matters to Jesus.

❋ Gaining wisdom matters to Jesus.

Busyness and Breathers

What are your favorite things to do with your time? Hang out with friends? Dance? Gymnastics? Soccer? Art? Reading? Music? Running? Video games? Crafts? Board games? Movies? With church and school and homework and activities and family and friends, there don't seem to be enough hours in the day! Oh, and what about sleep? Sleep needs to fit in there somewhere. And these days, everyone seems to be so busy—All. The. Time. Busy can be good, and busy can be bad—and it matters to Jesus how we spend our time.

Maybe you've heard someone in church talk about being a Mary type of person or a Martha type of person. In the Bible in Luke chapter 10, Jesus had a talk with a woman named Martha about being too busy to just relax and spend time listening to Him and learning from Him, like her sister Mary was doing. And here's the thing: Martha wasn't doing bad things with her time; she was doing *good* things— serving others and being a great hostess—but even the good things that keep us busy turn into bad ways to spend our time IF they are keeping us from spending time with Jesus.

Now as they went on their way, Jesus entered a village. And a woman named Martha welcomed him into her house. And she had a sister called Mary, who sat at the Lord's feet and listened to his teaching. But Martha was distracted with much serving. And she went up to him and said, "Lord, do you not care that my sister has left me to serve alone? Tell her then to help me." But the Lord answered her, "Martha, Martha, you are anxious and troubled about many things, but one thing is necessary. Mary has chosen the good portion, which will not be taken away from her."

LUKE 10:38–42 ESV

It's ginormously important to get in the habit now while you're young of making daily quiet time with Jesus. It matters so much to Him. Imagine if you have a friend who calls you her BFF and yet never talks to you, never listens to you, never sets aside any time to hang out with you. That's not much of a friend at all, is it? If you call Jesus your friend and Savior, make sure you are spending daily time with Him—*quiet* time as you pray and read His Word, so that you can learn to hear from Him.

Be wise and purposeful with your time, remembering that good things can turn into bad things if you don't focus on what's really important. For example, you can spend all kinds of time in church activities and helping with ministries. . .but never spend any time actually talking and listening to God and reading your Bible. And which is more important?

You can spend all kinds of time doing activities with your friends. . .but have no time to actually *be* a friend by listening to or praying with or keeping someone company who needs you. And which is more important?

You can spend hours at your desk trying to get your homework done. . .but your mind keeps wandering or you keep playing on your iPod and wasting your time. And which is more important?

Check out the following verses on using time, and ask God to help you spend every minute of your precious time wisely:

Look carefully then how you walk, not as unwise but as wise, making the best use of the time, because the days are evil. Therefore do not be foolish, but understand what the will of the Lord is.

EPHESIANS 5:15-17 ESV

"This is what the LORD of Heaven's Armies says: Look at what's happening to you! You have planted much but harvest little. You eat but are not satisfied. You drink but are still thirsty. You put on clothes but cannot keep warm. Your wages disappear as though you were putting them in pockets filled with holes! This is what the LORD of Heaven's Armies says: Look at what's happening to you! Now go up into the hills, bring down timber, and rebuild my house. Then I will take pleasure in it and be honored, says the LORD. You hoped for rich harvests, but they were poor. And when you brought your harvest home, I blew it away. Why? Because my house lies in ruins, says the LORD of Heaven's Armies, while all of you are busy building your own fine houses."

HAGGAI 1:5-9 NLT

We need to spend our time doing things that will matter for eternity, not just for this life, because like 1 John 2:17 (ESV) says, "The world is passing away along with its desires, but whoever does the will of God abides forever."

I'm a grown-up, and I need to review this chapter again and again. It's hard. Life fights us on this like crazy, with so much work to be done and so many activities and people and social media updates demanding our attention! But it's a battle worth fighting to keep your time prioritized with the things that are most important.

And don't forget that resting matters to Jesus. God created a whole day for it!

So God blessed the seventh day and made it holy, because on it God rested from all his work that he had done in creation.
GENESIS 2:3 ESV

Also, one of the Ten Commandments commands us to rest!

"Six days you shall work, but on the seventh day you shall rest."
EXODUS 34:21 ESV

Here are some more verses about resting from the Bible:

Then Jesus said, "Let's go off by
ourselves to a quiet place and rest awhile."
MARK 6:31 NLT

"Be still, and know that I am God."
PSALM 46:10 ESV

"Better to have one handful with quietness than two
handfuls with hard work and chasing the wind."
ECCLESIASTES 4:6 NLT

We need rest to recharge and be able to do the things God has created us to do and to share His love the way He wants us to and bring glory to Him. If we spend our time putting God first and asking for His help to plan our time, there will always be enough time and we will always find rest because Jesus said, "If you are tired from carrying heavy burdens, come to me and I will give you rest. Take the yoke I give you. Put it on your shoulders and learn from me. I am gentle and humble, and you will find rest. This yoke is easy to bear, and this burden is light" (Matthew 11:28–30 CEV).

It All Matters to Jesus

❋ How you spend your time matters to Jesus.

❋ Daily quiet time to pray matters to Jesus.

❋ Daily quiet time to read the Bible matters to Jesus.

❋ Daily quiet time to be still and listen for God matters to Jesus.

❋ Not being too busy matters to Jesus.

❋ Taking time to rest matters to Jesus.

❋ Balancing our activities with time to spend with God matters to Jesus.

Joy, Joy, Joy!

These days, I can't hear the word *happy* without the fun tune from *Despicable Me 2* going through my mind, and then suddenly I'm dancing around like a crazy yellow minion. Anyone else with me on this? I love that movie!

What does it take to make you happy? You'll have a different answer to that question than your best friend or your sister or your cousin because every person is so different. *Happy* is so subjective, meaning what makes one person happy doesn't make another person happy in the same way. *Happy* is also kind of fickle, meaning it's not consistent and it changes pretty easily. Think about the things that made you *so* happy a few years ago. Would they make you happy in the same way now? Some things might, but as you grow up and mature it takes different things to make you happy.

Our culture puts a lot of importance on being happy. Maybe for school you've even memorized the famous line from our great nation's Declaration of Independence about "life, liberty, and the pursuit of happiness."

You'll often hear people say, "I just want to be happy," like that's the very best and brightest goal of life. And of course it's a wonderful thing to be happy, but if you pursue only happiness, you'll never stop chasing it— because you'll never be satisfied. And Jesus wants you to be satisfied. It matters to Him that you have *joy*, not just happiness, and that joy comes from Him.

Happiness is based on circumstances, and circumstances can change so easily. Think about how happy you are when your mom fixes your favorite food for supper. Then think about how unhappy you feel with a sick stomach if you eat way too much of the very thing that made you so happy at first.

Think about how happy you were when you received everything you asked for on your Christmas list when you were five years old. Now think about how unhappy those same gifts for Christmas might make you because you've grown up a lot since then.

Joy is based on Jesus, and He never changes. Joy is not just nice, upbeat feelings based on the good things going on around you; joy is a state of being content, confident, steady, and full of hope and positivity, even in the worst of circumstances. Joy comes from knowing Jesus as Savior and knowing that He wins against all the awful stuff that happens in this world, that He will conquer it all and one day we will live in perfect happiness with Him in heaven, forever!

Read these verses about joy; then thank Jesus and ask Him to fill you every day with His joy. It's a zillion times better than just being happy.

Though you have not seen him, you love him;
and even though you do not see him now,
you believe in him and are filled with an inexpressible
and glorious joy, for you are receiving the end result
of your faith, the salvation of your souls.
1 PETER 1:8–9 NIV

A joyful heart is good medicine,
but a crushed spirit dries up the bones.
PROVERBS 17:22 ESV

*"So also you have sorrow now, but I will
see you again, and your hearts will rejoice,
and no one will take your joy from you."*

JOHN 16:22 ESV

*With all my heart, I will celebrate, and I can safely rest.
I am your chosen one. You won't leave me in the grave or
let my body decay. You have shown me the path to life,
and you make me glad by being near to me. Sitting at
your right side, I will always be joyful.*

PSALM 16:9-11 CEV

*Dear brothers and sisters, when troubles of any kind
come your way, consider it an opportunity for great
joy. For you know that when your faith is tested, your
endurance has a chance to grow. So let it grow, for when
your endurance is fully developed, you will be perfect
and complete, needing nothing.*

JAMES 1:2-4 NLT

*The hope of the righteous brings joy,
but the expectation of the wicked will perish.*

PROVERBS 10:28 ESV

Sing to the LORD, all you godly ones! Praise his holy name.
For his anger lasts only a moment, but his favor lasts
a lifetime! Weeping may last through the night,
but joy comes with the morning.

PSALM 30:4-5 NLT

This is the day that the LORD has made;
let us rejoice and be glad in it.

PSALM 118:24 ESV

You make known to me the path of life;
in your presence there is fullness of joy;
at your right hand are pleasures forevermore.

PSALM 16:11 ESV

May the God of hope fill you with all joy and
peace as you trust in him, so that you may
overflow with hope by the power of the Holy Spirit.

ROMANS 15:13 NIV

It All Matters to Jesus

❀ Joy matters more than happiness to Jesus.

❀ Finding your joy in Him matters to Jesus.

❀ Praising God and singing with joy matters to Jesus.

❀ Sharing your joy with others matters to Jesus.

A Tongue Twister:
Practice Pleasant Patience

Someday you'll probably have your own car, and you might want to design your own license plate. When I was in eighth grade, I (obviously) didn't own a car, but I had a cool English teacher who gave us an assignment to design a license plate and then write about what it meant. I still remember mine because I was rather proud of it—I H8 2 W8. I thought I was pretty clever, and I totally meant what it said: "I hate to wait."

Lots of years later, I still hate to wait sometimes. More often than I'd like to admit, in fact. But patience is part of the fruit of the Spirit. It should be plain to see in our lives if we've accepted the Holy Spirit, and it matters to Jesus if we practice patience.

How are you at waiting and being patient? Maybe there are some things you are fine waiting on. I'm always amazed that some people actually *enjoy* the wait in long lines at amusement parks or at stores for Black Friday shopping.

But there are all sorts of things that can make you feel impatient. Do your siblings take too much time in the bathroom in the mornings? Does Mom always seem to be forever cooking supper when your stomach is about to cave in from starvation? Do the minutes of the school day sometimes tick by in superslow motion? Does the countdown to summer break take an absolute eternity?

What's your attitude while you wait for these things? Does it need an adjustment? Do you stay calm and kind, or do you start to complain and freak out and get irritable and whiny?

And how do you feel when people are impatient with you? It's not fun, is it? But what about when others show you patience? That's nice, right? So, just like the Golden Rule says to "do unto others," you need to treat others with the patience that you know is nice to receive. It's hard, believe me I know, but it's the right thing to do.

Maybe there are big things that make you feel impatient. Have you been praying for what seems like forever for a parent to find a new job? Or for a relative to be healed from cancer? Or for a bully to leave you alone?

In all the ways that need your patience, hang in there. Ask God to keep you cool when impatience threatens to overheat your temper or cause you to doubt Him or make you want to give up. Check out these verses to help you stay focused and able to practice pleasant patience. (Can you say that out loud? It's quite a tongue twister!)

My friends, be patient until the Lord returns. Think of farmers who wait patiently for the spring and summer rains to make their valuable crops grow. Be patient like those farmers and don't give up. The Lord will soon be here!
JAMES 5:7–8 CEV

Rejoice in our confident hope.
Be patient in trouble, and keep on praying.
ROMANS 12:12 NLT

Be patient with everyone.
1 THESSALONIANS 5:14 CEV

*But if we look forward to something we don't yet have,
we must wait patiently and confidently.*
ROMANS 8:25 NLT

*He will give eternal life to everyone who has patiently
done what is good in the hope of receiving glory,
honor, and life that lasts forever.*
ROMANS 2:7 CEV

*The LORD is kind to everyone who trusts and obeys him.
It is good to wait patiently for the LORD to save us.*
LAMENTATIONS 3:25-26 CEV

*Be patient and trust the LORD. Don't let it bother you
when all goes well for those who do sinful things.*
PSALM 37:7 CEV

Patiently put up with each other and love each other.
EPHESIANS 4:2 CEV

*But they who wait for the LORD shall renew their strength;
they shall mount up with wings like eagles; they shall run
and not be weary; they shall walk and not faint.*
ISAIAH 40:31 ESV

Patience is better than pride.
ECCLESIASTES 7:8 NLT

It All Matters to Jesus

❋ Learning to be patient matters to Jesus.

❋ Having a good attitude while you're waiting matters to Jesus.

❋ Having patience with other people matters to Jesus.

❋ Letting God teach you while you're waiting on an answer to prayer matters to Jesus.

❋ Learning to trust God while you wait matters to Jesus.

Peace Out

What are some of the things you fight most about with your siblings? I have two big brothers who used to sit on me when I tried to get the remote for the TV, and my sister and I fought over toys and clothes and who got to ride in the front seat of the car. I bet those kinds of fights with siblings are still pretty common today. Can you relate? Or maybe you sometimes fight with your friends over choosing what movie to watch or what game to play or activity to do. Or with your parents over chores or getting your homework done on time.

Here's a verse that talks about what causes fights:

Why do you fight and argue with each other? Isn't it because you are full of selfish desires that fight to control your body?
JAMES 4:1 CEV

We are all full of selfish desires, and when we let them control us, then we usually end up in conflict with someone because eventually our selfish desire is going to clash with someone else's selfish desire.

135

For example, if there's one *last* chocolate chip cookie (or whatever treat you like best) sitting on a plate on the counter and you and your brother both reach for it at the same moment. . .suddenly you're shoving and yelling and wrestling and mad—all because of a cookie.

Or a selfish desire can clash with the rules and get you into conflict—like if you know it's your turn to let the dog out and feed him, but you just don't want to pause the movie you're watching to take care of him, so then the dog pees all over your sister's shoes and now your sister looks ready to pull all your hair out.

Or a selfish desire can clash with the requirements and get you into conflict—like if you blow off your history assignment because you just don't feel like doing it and you get an F and now your parents and teacher are less than thrilled with you and you're grounded and you're mad.

You get the idea.

Fighting is usually caused by people being selfish—and I know, I know, it's not always your fault or your selfishness that causes a fight. Sometimes the fights come to you. But whether you start conflict or not, you can always ask Jesus to help you *finish* it, because peace matters to Jesus.

Peace is a fruit of the Spirit (see Galatians 5:22), meaning it's something others can see in our lives when we've asked Jesus to be our Savior and have the Holy Spirit living in us. The Bible also says about peace:

If possible, so far as it depends on you,
live peaceably with all.
ROMANS 12:18 ESV

Turn away from evil and do good.
Search for peace, and work to maintain it.
1 PETER 3:11 NLT

"God blesses those who work for peace,
for they will be called the children of God."
MATTHEW 5:9 NLT

Work at living in peace with everyone, and work at living
a holy life, for those who are not holy will not see the Lord.
HEBREWS 12:14 NLT

Being a peacemaker doesn't mean you have to be a wimp or let yourself be bullied when a fight comes to you that you didn't start. But it means that you do your part to make things right and peaceful. Here are some verses on how to make up when you're in the middle of a fight.

Be kind to one another, tenderhearted,
forgiving one another, as God in Christ forgave you.
EPHESIANS 4:32 ESV

Put up with each other, and forgive anyone who
does you wrong, just as Christ has forgiven you.
Love is more important than anything else.
It is what ties everything completely together.
COLOSSIANS 3:13–14 CEV

"If another believer sins against you, go privately and
point out the offense. If the other person listens and
confesses it, you have won that person back. But if you are
unsuccessful, take one or two others with you and go back
again, so that everything you say may be confirmed by
two or three witnesses. If the person still refuses to listen,
take your case to the church."
MATTHEW 18:15–17 NLT

For the stuff that is unfair, the fights you didn't start, the injustice that's been done to you, the stuff you just can't seem to get closure or a peaceful conclusion to, you leave that up to God. God is not some weak and wimpy old man in the sky. He is a righteous, holy, and just God. He sees all and knows all, and when you are living your life to obey Him, He will fight for you and He will make all things right for you—not always exactly when you want Him to, but He will do it exactly at the right time that is best for you.

Ask God to bless everyone who mistreats you. Ask him to bless them and not to curse them. When others are happy, be happy with them, and when they are sad, be sad. Be friendly with everyone. Don't be proud and feel that you are smarter than others. Make friends with ordinary people. Don't mistreat someone who has mistreated you. But try to earn the respect of others, and do your best to live at peace with everyone.
ROMANS 12:14-18 CEV

Dear friends, don't try to get even. Let God take revenge. In the Scriptures the Lord says, "I am the one to take revenge and pay them back."
ROMANS 12:19 CEV

Strive to be a peacemaker and let God do the fighting!

It All Matters to Jesus

❈ Being a peacemaker matters to Jesus.

❈ Living in peace with others matters to Jesus.

❈ Controlling the selfishness that often causes fighting matters to Jesus.

❈ Trusting God to help you make peace matters to Jesus.

❈ Loving and forgiving matters to Jesus.

❈ Searching for peace and working hard to keep peace matters to Jesus.

Peace In

We've talked about keeping peace around you on the outside, now what about on the inside? It matters a lot to Jesus that you have perfect peace in your heart and mind. Do you ever feel overly anxious and worried about things? I don't mean just the usual worried about a test coming up or worried that you're going to be late to school one too many times. I'm talking about sick-to-your-stomach, keep-you-awake-at-night, all-the-time kind of worry. It seems like more and more people have what's called anxiety problems—you hear doctors on TV and in magazines and on blogs talk a lot about it these days.

Maybe it's not something you're dealing with at your age, but if not now, someday you might. I'm not trying to scare you. I just want to make sure you know one way, *the best way*, that you can fight anxiety and have peace—by asking for help from the God who made you and loves you more than anyone else and who is the God of all peace (see Isaiah 9:6 and Romans 15:33) and comfort (see 2 Corinthians 1:3).

God's power to help us with our anxiety is bigger and better than anything any medical professional here on earth can do. Let me be clear: I am not saying that medical help is never necessary for anxiety. It absolutely is sometimes. But for Christians who have the Holy Spirit, first God wants us to bring our anxiety problems to Him and let Him help. The Bible tells us so again and again:

You will keep in perfect peace all who trust in you, all whose thoughts are fixed on you! Trust in the LORD always, for the LORD GOD is the eternal Rock.

ISAIAH 26:3-4 NLT

Don't worry about anything, but pray about everything. With thankful hearts offer up your prayers and requests to God. Then, because you belong to Christ Jesus, God will bless you with peace that no one can completely understand. And this peace will control the way you think and feel.

PHILIPPIANS 4:6-7 CEV

And let the peace of Christ rule in your hearts.

COLOSSIANS 3:15 ESV

I tell you not to worry about your life. Don't worry about having something to eat, drink, or wear. Isn't life more than food or clothing? Look at the birds in the sky! They don't plant or harvest. They don't even store grain in barns. Yet your Father in heaven takes care of them. Aren't you worth more than birds?

Can worry make you live longer? Why worry about clothes? Look how the wild flowers grow. They don't work hard to make their clothes. But I tell you that Solomon with all his wealth wasn't as well clothed as one of them. God gives such beauty to everything that grows in the fields, even though it is here today and thrown into a fire tomorrow. He will surely do even more for you!

Why do you have such little faith?

Don't worry and ask yourselves, "Will we have anything to eat? Will we have anything to drink? Will we have any clothes to wear?" Only people who don't know God are always worrying about such things. Your Father in heaven knows that you need all of these. But more than anything else, put God's work first and do what he wants. Then the other things will be yours as well. Don't worry about tomorrow. It will take care of itself. You have enough to worry about today.

MATTHEW 6:25-34 CEV

Humble yourselves, therefore, under God's mighty hand, that he may lift you up in due time. Cast all your anxiety on him because he cares for you.

1 Peter 5:6–7 niv

"Peace I leave with you; my peace I give you. I do not give to you as the world gives. Do not let your hearts be troubled and do not be afraid."

John 14:27 niv

"I have told you these things, so that in me you may have peace. In this world you will have trouble. But take heart! I have overcome the world."

John 16:33 niv

For God is not a God of confusion but of peace.

1 Corinthians 14:33 esv

In peace I will lie down and sleep, for you alone, O Lord, will keep me safe.

Psalm 4:8 nlt

Those who love your instructions have great peace and do not stumble. I long for your rescue, Lord, so I have obeyed your commands. I have obeyed your laws, for I love them very much. Yes, I obey your commandments and laws because you know everything I do.

Psalm 119:165–168 nlt

You will walk safely and never stumble; you will rest without a worry and sleep soundly. So don't be afraid of sudden disasters or storms that strike those who are evil. You can be sure that the L<small>ORD</small> will protect you from harm.

PROVERBS 3:23-26 CEV

My health may fail, and my spirit may grow weak, but God remains the strength of my heart; he is mine forever.

PSALM 73:26 NLT

Whenever you might find yourself overwhelmed with worry and stress and anxiety, read these verses, memorize them, recite them over and over. Let Jesus, the Prince of Peace, calm you and steady you, and remember that someday soon we will live in peace with Him FOREVER without a worry or care ever again.

"Do not let your hearts be troubled. You believe in God; believe also in me. My Father's house has many rooms; if that were not so, would I have told you that I am going there to prepare a place for you? And if I go and prepare a place for you, I will come back and take you to be with me that you also may be where I am."

JOHN 14:1-3 NIV

It All Matters to Jesus

✳ All your worries matter to Jesus.

✳ Giving you peace on the inside matters to Jesus.

✳ Being your peace matters to Jesus.

✳ Giving you peaceful sleep matters to Jesus.

✳ Helping you feel safe matters to Jesus.

✳ Letting God have power over your anxiety matters to Jesus.

Don't Be a Meanie!

Have you ever gotten stuck in line at one of those
self-checkout stations at the grocery store? I had
an experience once when I was trying to buy some
fruit that wouldn't ring up correctly, and all of a
sudden the machine was yelling at me over and over,
"Move your Asian pears! Move your Asian pears!"
in a loud robotic voice, with a line of customers
behind me looking pretty grumpy. Um, can you say
AWKWARD? Now that I look back, it's superfunny,
though.

Ever since that experience, I remember it and
laugh to myself when I'm stuck in line behind people
who are having a similar problem at the grocery
store—and I act kindly toward them, even if it means
I'm stuck in line a little longer. I smile and show them
it's not a big deal if I have to wait a little extra while
they get the problem figured out. I've been in their
shoes before. I'll help if I can, and at the very least
I'll be pleasant and not make the situation worse by
being grumpy and rude.

I've noticed recently how unkind people can be
while they wait in line at a busy store or in traffic, and
it's so frustrating and just plain mean! Decide now
while you're young not to be one of those people.
Choose to be a person who shows kindness at every
opportunity. Hold doors for people. Smile and be

friendly. Go out of your way to help someone. If you see someone behind you in line who has just a couple of items and you have a whole cartful, let that person go ahead of you. Wait for things patiently.

There are a zillion kind things you can do for others, and they don't have to be big things. Make a list of the little things you could do around the house or at school or when you're out and about that would show kindness to others.

One of the simplest ways to be kind is with encouragement. Have you ever been like Alexander—having a terrible, horrible, no good, very bad day—but then just a simple, kind, and encouraging word helped change everything?

Maybe your teacher told you what a great job you did on your project, or a friend complimented your outfit, or your mom noticed how nicely you cleaned up your room and left you a thank-you note for it in your lunch box. It feels great, doesn't it? And it feels even better to be the giver of those kind words. To watch a person's face light up with a smile as that person feels encouraged and appreciated is priceless! But it doesn't have to be in person; just a simple e-mail or text message to let someone know you're thinking of her and praying for her can mean so much to someone going through a rough time. Start the habit now of being a person who looks for the good in others and encourages them and thanks them for it.

And be sure to try this—even when you don't *feel* like being kind, be kind anyway, and just watch how it changes you and those around you.

Kindness in both our actions and our words matters to Jesus. It's part of the fruit of the Spirit, which shows that we are true Christians.

But the fruit of the Spirit is love, joy, peace, patience, kindness, goodness, faithfulness, gentleness, self-control.
GALATIANS 5:22–23 ESV

The Bible also says all this about kindness:

Be kind to one another, tenderhearted, forgiving one another, as God in Christ forgave you.
EPHESIANS 4:32 ESV

"But love your enemies, do good to them, and lend to them without expecting to get anything back. Then your reward will be great, and you will be children of the Most High, because he is kind to the ungrateful and wicked."
LUKE 6:35 NIV

Your kindness will reward you,
but your cruelty will destroy you.

Proverbs 11:17 nlt

Since God chose you to be the holy people he loves,
you must clothe yourselves with tenderhearted mercy,
kindness, humility, gentleness, and patience.

Colossians 3:12 nlt

Teach those who are rich in this world not to be proud
and not to trust in their money, which is so unreliable.
Their trust should be in God, who richly gives us all we
need for our enjoyment. Tell them to use their money
to do good. They should be rich in good works and
generous to those in need, always being ready to
share with others. By doing this they will be storing
up their treasure as a good foundation for the future
so that they may experience true life.

1 Timothy 6:17–19 nlt

Dear brothers and sisters,
never get tired of doing good.
2 Thessalonians 3:13 nlt

We should help others do what is
right and build them up in the Lord.
Romans 15:2 nlt

Children, you show love for others by truly helping them,
and not merely by talking about it.
1 John 3:18 cev

It All Matters to Jesus

❀ Being kind to others matters to Jesus.

❀ Encouraging others matters to Jesus.

❀ Holding doors for others matters to Jesus.

❀ Being polite to others matters to Jesus.

❀ Smiling at others matters to Jesus.

❀ Letting others go first matters to Jesus.

❀ Being kind even when you don't feel like it matters to Jesus.

From Another World

Do you like the movie *Lilo and Stitch*? I love it! Poor Lilo is so funny and misunderstood, and Stitch is such a crazy but cute little alien guy. The lovely setting of Hawaii (even in cartoon form) is so nice to watch, too. I think it would be amazing to live somewhere I could walk to beautiful sands and warm ocean waters. Ahhhh. . .

Anyway, back to aliens. Did you know that as a Christian you're supposed to be like an alien? I don't mean you're supposed to start growing extra eyeballs or turn green or start communicating with clicks and screeches through baby monitors.

I mean *alien* as in *a stranger* like this definition from *Merriam-Webster*: "belonging or relating to another person, place, or thing."

And like this verse of the Bible which uses the word *alien*: "Beloved, I urge you as aliens and strangers to abstain from fleshly lusts which wage war against the soul. Keep your behavior excellent among the Gentiles, so that in the thing in which they slander you as evildoers, they may because of your good deeds, as they observe them, glorify God in the day of visitation" (1 Peter 2:11–12 NASB).

153

Basically, as someone who loves and follows Jesus, you are supposed to be an alien or a stranger to this world because you know that you are just here on this earth for a short time compared to where you ultimately belong—with God in heaven forever. But while you're here, the things you do differently than the world, the strange "alien" ways about you, will show others that you follow and worship the one true God.

It means when most people in the world are looking out for themselves, you're looking out for others first.

It means when most people in the world say it's okay to cheat and lie a little, you're being honest.

It means when most people in the world are turning away from the Bible, you're sticking to it.

It means when most people in the world think going to church is a waste of time, you keep on going.

It means when most people in the world say any type of TV or movies is okay, you are careful what you watch.

It means when most people in the world say there is no God, you keep living for Him.

It means that compared to most people in the world, the people around you see real differences in the way you live your life.

It means you strive to do everything with excellence because everything you do is for God:

But since you excel in everything—in faith, in speech, in knowledge, in complete earnestness and in the love we have kindled in you—see that you also excel in this grace of giving.
2 CORINTHIANS 8:7 NIV

Work with enthusiasm, as though you were working for the Lord rather than for people. Remember that the Lord will reward each one of us for the good we do.
EPHESIANS 6:7-8 NLT

By his divine power, God has given us everything we need for living a godly life. We have received all of this by coming to know him, the one who called us to himself by means of his marvelous glory and excellence. And because of his glory and excellence, he has given us great and precious promises. These are the promises that enable you to share his divine nature and escape the world's corruption caused by human desires. In view of all this, make every effort to respond to God's promises. Supplement your faith with a generous provision of moral excellence, and moral excellence with knowledge, and knowledge with self-control, and self-control with patient endurance, and patient endurance with godliness, and godliness with brotherly affection, and brotherly affection with love for everyone.
2 PETER 1:3-7 NLT

It means you strive to do everything with integrity:

Whoever walks in integrity walks securely, but he who makes his ways crooked will be found out.
PROVERBS 10:9 ESV

Better is a poor man who walks in his integrity than a rich man who is crooked in his ways.
PROVERBS 28:6 ESV

*If you do the right thing, honesty will
be your guide. But if you are crooked,
you will be trapped by your own dishonesty.*
PROVERBS 11:3 CEV

*Better is a poor person who walks in his integrity
than one who is crooked in speech and is a fool.*
PROVERBS 19:1 ESV

Show yourself in all respects to be a model of good works.
TITUS 2:7 ESV

And it means you strive to live a holy life:

*Be alert and think straight. Put all your hope in how kind
God will be to you when Jesus Christ appears. Behave
like obedient children. Don't let your lives be controlled
by your desires, as they used to be. Always live as God's
holy people should, because God is the one who chose
you, and he is holy. That's why the Scriptures say,
"I am the holy God, and you must be holy too."*
1 PETER 1:13–16 CEV

*We should stay away from everything that keeps our
bodies and spirits from being clean. We should
honor God and try to be completely like him.*
2 CORINTHIANS 7:1 CEV

Work at living in peace with everyone, and work at living a holy life, for those who are not holy will not see the Lord.
HEBREWS 12:14 NLT

But you are God's chosen and special people. You are a group of royal priests and a holy nation. God has brought you out of darkness into his marvelous light.
1 PETER 2:9 CEV

God has called us to live holy lives, not impure lives.
1 THESSALONIANS 4:7 NLT

In a wealthy home some utensils are made of gold and silver, and some are made of wood and clay. The expensive utensils are used for special occasions, and the cheap ones are for everyday use. If you keep yourself pure, you will be a special utensil for honorable use. Your life will be clean, and you will be ready for the Master to use you for every good work.
2 TIMOTHY 2:20-21 NLT

So embrace your "inner alien" and be so different from the world that others see that difference and want to know more about Jesus, too!

It All Matters to Jesus

❋ Being very different from the world matters to Jesus.

❋ Being honest when others are lying matters to Jesus.

❋ Reading the Bible when others have stopped matters to Jesus.

❋ Going to church when so many don't anymore matters to Jesus.

❋ Living a holy life matters to Jesus.

❋ Being careful what you watch and listen to and read matters to Jesus.

❋ Having integrity matters to Jesus.

Don't Eat All the Chocolate

I have a hard time around chocolate. It's *soooooo* good that I forget not to eat too much sometimes. Okay, *a lot* of the time! Do you have a favorite food you go crazy for? Is it candy or chips or pizza or something else? But what happens if you eat way too much of that favorite food? Sometimes the result is not pretty. We have to control how much we eat at one time or we get sick. Self-control matters for a lot of things in our lives, not just food.

For example, how much TV should you watch?

How much time should you spend on the computer?

How much time should you spend texting your friends?

How much time do you need to spend on your homework?

How much time do you need to do your chores?

How much time do you need to sleep at night?

How much time do you need to spend being active and getting exercise rather than just chilling on the couch?

All these things need self-control to manage the hours in the day and the things you need to do to be healthy and meet your responsibilities.

You also need self-control over your tongue—the things you say.

Watching what you say can save you a lot of trouble.
PROVERBS 21:23 CEV

And you need self-control over your emotions and reactions.

My dear friends, you should be quick to listen and slow to speak or to get angry.
JAMES 1:19 CEV

And you need self-control over your thoughts.

Finally, my friends, keep your minds on whatever is true, pure, right, holy, friendly, and proper. Don't ever stop thinking about what is truly worthwhile and worthy of praise.
PHILIPPIANS 4:8 CEV

When you're young, you're still learning a lot about self-control and hopefully a grown-up is helping you figure it out, but each year you get older, you're more and more responsible. And don't ever forget that you're never alone. The Holy Spirit is with you and will help you keep control. Just ask Him!

Read and think about these verses to help you!

A person without self-control
is like a city with broken-down walls.
PROVERBS 25:28 NLT

Do your best to improve your faith. You can do this by
adding goodness, understanding, self-control, patience,
devotion to God, concern for others, and love.
2 PETER 1:5–7 CEV

Be self-controlled and sober-minded
for the sake of your prayers.
1 PETER 4:7 ESV

For God gave us a spirit not of fear
but of power and love and self-control.
2 TIMOTHY 1:7 ESV

It All Matters to Jesus

❀ Self-control matters to Jesus.

❀ Being careful what you say matters to Jesus.

❀ Eating healthy foods in healthy ways matters to Jesus.

❀ Having enough time for schoolwork matters to Jesus.

❀ Getting enough sleep at night matters to Jesus.

❀ Exercising your body in a healthy way matters to Jesus.

❀ Making time to help with chores matters to Jesus.

❀ Having control over your tongue matters to Jesus.

❀ Having control over your thoughts matters to Jesus.

Strengths and Weaknesses

I remember when I was in the third grade, I told some friends I was going to be a superstar gymnast and get all the way to the Olympics—the problem was, I'd never had any lessons, and other than being able to do splits and cartwheels okay, I was not really any good at gymnastics. I sure needed a reality check! LOL!

I eventually figured out that my dream of being an Olympic gymnast just wasn't going to happen for me, and that was okay. Gymnastics was not a strength God had given me. What He had given me was a gift for reading and writing and learning, and I began to focus on what I could do with that. I started dreaming of working for a Christian publishing company, and now I do exactly what I dreamed of!

Maybe gymnastics is something *you* are great at. Or soccer or dance or running or drawing or music or public speaking or making new friends or whatever!

God has given you a unique set of strengths and talents, and it matters that you figure out what they are and then use them for God, doing your very best at them as a way to praise and worship Him! Do you know that praise and worship doesn't mean just singing time at church? Praise and worship can be anything you do that pleases God and gives Him the glory. It's a way of life—giving your life to God and living your life for God, in a way that everything you do tries to honor Him.

And so, dear brothers and sisters, I plead with you to give your bodies to God because of all he has done for you. Let them be a living and holy sacrifice—the kind he will find acceptable. This is truly the way to worship him.
ROMANS 12:1 NLT

Strengths aren't just the activities and hobbies and sports we're good at. We've all been given spiritual gifts, too.

Each of you has been blessed with one of God's many wonderful gifts to be used in the service of others. So use your gift well. If you have the gift of speaking, preach God's message. If you have the gift of helping others, do it with the strength that God supplies. Everything should be done in a way that will bring honor to God because of Jesus Christ, who is glorious and powerful forever.

1 PETER 4:10–11 CEV

In his grace, God has given us different gifts for doing certain things well. So if God has given you the ability to prophesy, speak out with as much faith as God has given you. If your gift is serving others, serve them well. If you are a teacher, teach well. If your gift is to encourage others, be encouraging. If it is giving, give generously. If God has given you leadership ability, take the responsibility seriously. And if you have a gift for showing kindness to others, do it gladly.

ROMANS 12:6–8 NLT

Just like everyone has strengths, that means the opposite is true—everyone has weaknesses. But do you know weaknesses don't have to be a bad thing? The Bible says that when we are weak, we are strong. That's kind of confusing, huh? Like a paradox.

Here's the scripture it comes from: "Three times I begged the Lord to make this suffering go away. But he replied, 'My kindness is all you need. My power is strongest when you are weak.' So if Christ keeps giving me his power, I will gladly brag about how weak I am. Yes, I am glad to be weak or insulted or mistreated or to have troubles and sufferings, if it is for Christ. Because when I am weak, I am strong" (2 Corinthians 12:8–10 CEV).

It means that the things we are weak at are what make us depend on God more. We need His help more with the things we're not good at, so we ask Him more and lean on Him more, and in the end that makes us stronger—because it's far better to be completely weak and dependent on God than it is to focus only on our strength and depend on just ourselves.

So, figure out your strengths and don't be frustrated by your weaknesses. Use both of them to worship God and let Him shine in your life!

It All Matters to Jesus

❀ Your strengths matter to Jesus.

❀ Your weaknesses matter to Jesus.

❀ Using your strengths for God matters to Jesus.

❀ Letting God help you in your weaknesses matters to Jesus.

Constant Conversation

Are you quiet in general, or are you mostly a talker? Or does it depend on where you are and who you're with? Maybe you're quiet at school or church or in a group but at home or one-on-one with someone you could talk all day.

Whom do you love to talk to the most? Your BFF or a family member? Or maybe even your pet? My dog is fun to talk to. He's a good listener and cocks his head so cute just like he's trying to understand.

Do you know who the best listener is and who's always available and who wishes you'd never stop talking to Him? You've probably guessed it! God. And while He was here on earth, Jesus taught about how we should pray because it matters so much to Him that we communicate regularly, constantly with Him!

Here is the Lord's Prayer, which is probably familiar to you, but maybe not in this version:

When you pray, don't be like those show-offs who love to stand up and pray in the meeting places and on the street corners. They do this just to look good. I can assure you that they already have their reward. When you pray, go into a room alone and close the door. Pray to your Father in private. He knows what is done in private, and he will reward you. When you pray, don't talk on and on as people do who don't know God. They think God likes to hear long prayers. Don't be like them. Your Father knows what you need before you ask. You should pray like this: Our Father in heaven, help us to honor your name. Come and set up your kingdom, so that everyone on earth will obey you, as you are obeyed in heaven. Give us our food for today. Forgive us for doing wrong, as we forgive others. Keep us from being tempted and protect us from evil.

MATTHEW 6:5-13 CEV

This is a model of prayer that Jesus gave us, showing us how to pray sincerely, with praise and honor to God, asking that His will be done first and foremost, asking for just what we need for each day, asking for forgiveness of sins and help to forgive others, and asking for protection against sin and against evil.

So, is this the only prayer we should ever say, and just recite it word for word? No, that's not what this means because the Bible also tells us other ways to pray.

The Bible tells us to pray for our salvation and for others to be saved, too:

Please, Lord, please save us.
Please, Lord, please give us success.
PSALM 118:25 NLT

Dear friends, my greatest wish and my prayer
to God is for the people of Israel to be saved.
ROMANS 10:1 CEV

The Bible says not to worry about anything but tell God all of our needs:

Don't worry about anything, but pray about everything.
With thankful hearts offer up your prayers and requests to
God. Then, because you belong to Christ Jesus, God will
bless you with peace that no one can completely understand.
And this peace will control the way you think and feel.
PHILIPPIANS 4:6-7 CEV

The Bible tells us to pray for others:

First of all, I ask you to pray for everyone. Ask God to help and bless them all, and tell God how thankful you are for each of them. Pray for kings and others in power, so that we may live quiet and peaceful lives as we worship and honor God. This kind of prayer is good, and it pleases God our Savior. God wants everyone to be saved.

1 TIMOTHY 2:1-4 CEV

Therefore confess your sins to each other and pray for each other so that you may be healed. The prayer of a righteous person is powerful and effective.

JAMES 5:16 NIV

The Bible tells us to pray for wisdom:

If any of you need wisdom, you should ask God, and it will be given to you. God is generous and won't correct you for asking.

JAMES 1:5 CEV

You can pray anywhere, anytime because God is always with you through the Holy Spirit, and even when you don't know what to pray for, pray anyway because:

In certain ways we are weak, but the Spirit is here to help us. For example, when we don't know what to pray for, the Spirit prays for us in ways that cannot be put into words. All of our thoughts are known to God. He can understand what is in the mind of the Spirit, as the Spirit prays for God's people.
ROMANS 8:26-27 CEV

Most importantly, don't ever stop praying. Keep in constant communication with God so the He can help you with each and every moment because it all matters to Him!

Never stop praying.
1 THESSALONIANS 5:17 CEV

It All Matters to Jesus

❀ Praying without bragging about it matters to Jesus.

❀ Praying for God's will matters to Jesus.

❀ Praying for others matters to Jesus.

❀ Praying for wisdom matters to Jesus.

❀ Sharing all your needs and worries and requests with God in prayer matters to Jesus.

❀ Constantly praying matters to Jesus.

The "B" Word

"I'm sooo booooo-ooooored!" Do you ever say that in a long whiny voice to anyone who will listen? Maybe in the middle of summer on a rainy day and there's no one around to hang out with and you can't go outside and you've read all the books in the house and watched all the good movies?

I used to whine about how bored I was when I was young, and I learned very quickly that if I said the "B" word to my mom, I would soon have lots and lots of chores to keep me busy. I laugh about it with her now, and it was a really good lesson for me to learn. The truth is, I think Christians especially should never be bored. We might feel bored for a minute or two, but then we can turn that boredom into action. There is always, always, *always* something we can do to be helpful or encouraging or productive in a way that honors God.

Maybe you don't think it sounds like fun at first, but if you choose to do it anyway, you might start to feel differently. You can help with chores that get overlooked sometimes—maybe cleaning out the fridge to help your mom. I know, I know—that totally doesn't sound very fun, but crank up some music and make it fun! Maybe you're sick of doing craft projects, but if you thought of a new person who could use some encouragement with a homemade card from you, you'd be interested again in crafting. Maybe your toys and stuffed animals feel old and boring, so you could spend some time going through them to give some away to others who might need them. Or see if you can volunteer at a secondhand store that helps others in need.

Boredom is often related to laziness, and God's Word tells us very strongly *not* to be lazy. Check it out:

> *Lazy people want much but get little,*
> *but those who work hard will prosper.*
> PROVERBS 13:4 NLT

> *"The one who is unwilling to work shall not eat."*
> 2 THESSALONIANS 3:10 NIV

Lazy people are soon poor;
hard workers get rich.
PROVERBS 10:4 NLT

A lazy person is as bad as
someone who destroys things.
PROVERBS 18:9 NLT

Do not love sleep or you will grow poor.
PROVERBS 20:13 NIV

Work hard and become a leader;
be lazy and become a slave.
PROVERBS 12:24 NLT

So when you feel those words—*I'm bored*—coming out of your mouth, stop them before they launch off your lips! Bust that boredom by asking God, "What could I do right now to be productive, helpful, encouraging, and smart with my time?" He will always help you find the answer!

It All Matters to Jesus

❋ Not being lazy matters to Jesus.

❋ Being willing to work hard matters to Jesus.

❋ Turning boredom into action matters to Jesus.

❋ Using extra time to help and encourage others matters to Jesus.

Hold On Lightly

What's your bedroom like? Are you messy or a neat freak? Is everything organized or in a jumble? Do you have toys and games and clothes and books in your room? A little or a lot? And how do you feel about your stuff? Is it easy to share and let others use your stuff, or do you hold on pretty tightly and protectively to it?

It can be hard to have a good balance of wanting to keep your things and keep them nice, yet always being generous and willing to share as the Bible says in 1 Timothy 6:18. The key is remembering that everything you have is a gift from God. The Bible says, "Every good and perfect gift comes down from the Father" (James 1:17 CEV).

"Wait, what?" you might say. "My parents gave me my iPad, and my grandparents gave me this bracelet, and I bought these cool shoes with my own money." But 1 Corinthians 4:7 (NLT) says, "What do you have that God hasn't given you? And if everything you have is from God, why boast as though it were not a gift?"

Yes, your gifts may be given to you by family members and you buy things with your own money, but who gives each person life and the ability to work and earn money and pay for things? God does. Ultimately, everything good comes from Him!

And a guy named Job in the Bible (maybe you've heard his story of riches to rags?) said, "We bring nothing at birth; we take nothing with us at death. The LORD alone gives and takes. Praise the name of the LORD!" (Job 1:21 CEV).

Because that is the truth, God wants you to hold not tightly but *lightly* to the things He has given you. I've heard it described that you can't open your hand to receive a new gift from God if you won't let go of the things He's already given you. Your hands can't fit everything at once. Neither can your life! So give and give and then give some more!

Ask God to show you every single day how He wants you to be generous—with your stuff, with your money, with your time, with your talents, with any of the perfect gifts He has given you.

If you start this habit while you're young, you will live a lifetime of generosity and you'll find that even while you're giving constantly, you'll be receiving so much more in all types of blessings—some you've never even dreamed of!

There are many, many verses in the Bible about giving. It's so important to God. Here are just a few. Read them again and again and let them inspire you to live a generous life:

"Give, and you will receive. Your gift will return to you in full—pressed down, shaken together to make room for more, running over, and poured into your lap. The amount you give will determine the amount you get back."
LUKE 6:38 NLT

Remember that our Lord Jesus said, "More blessings come from giving than from receiving."
ACTS 20:35 CEV

Give freely and become more wealthy; be stingy and lose everything. The generous will prosper; those who refresh others will themselves be refreshed.
PROVERBS 11:24–25 NLT

While Jesus was in the Temple, he watched the rich people dropping their gifts in the collection box. Then a poor widow came by and dropped in two small coins. "I tell you the truth," Jesus said, "this poor widow has given more than all the rest of them. For they have given a tiny part of their surplus, but she, poor as she is, has given everything she has."

LUKE 21:1-4 NLT

Teach those who are rich in this world not to be proud and not to trust in their money, which is so unreliable. Their trust should be in God, who richly gives us all we need for our enjoyment. Tell them to use their money to do good. They should be rich in good works and generous to those in need, always being ready to share with others. By doing this they will be storing up their treasure as a good foundation for the future so that they may experience true life.

1 TIMOTHY 6:17-19 NLT

Remember this—a farmer who plants only a few seeds will get a small crop. But the one who plants generously will get a generous crop. You must each decide in your heart how much to give. And don't give reluctantly or in response to pressure. "For God loves a person who gives cheerfully." And God will generously provide all you need. Then you will always have everything you need and plenty left over to share with others. As the Scriptures say, "They share freely and give generously to the poor. Their good deeds will be remembered forever." For God is the one who provides seed for the farmer and then bread to eat. In the same way, he will provide and increase your resources and then produce a great harvest of generosity in you.

2 CORINTHIANS 9:6–10 NLT

It All Matters to Jesus

❋ Generosity matters to Jesus.

❋ Holding on lightly to your stuff matters to Jesus.

❋ Being willing to give good things away matters to Jesus.

❋ Giving your time matters to Jesus.

❋ Giving your money matters to Jesus.

❋ Sharing your talents matters to Jesus.

❋ Blessing you with new good things matters to Jesus.

Content, Not Comparing

I have a confession.

Every time I go to the beach, I get really jealous of those who live near it. I *adore* the beach! I love how soothing it is to hear the waves. I love the simple fun of just digging in the sand, collecting seashells. I love the salty breeze. I love to read on the beach and walk on the beach and watch those cute little birds that scurry along the edges of the waves as they go in and out. And I wish I could walk on the beach. Every. Single. Day.

I also have similar feelings and many reasons for why I love Disney World. And I think that people who live near the beach and near Disney World must be the luckiest people in the world!

So every time I go on vacation to Florida, I come home thinking, *We should move. We should just do it!*

I start feeling like maybe I don't like where we live, even though I have a nice house and dear family and friends living close-by and a wonderful church and a great community. Basically, I start to feel so discontent with all the wonderful blessings God has given me and jealous over what those who live in Florida do have. And that's not good. It's even one of the Ten Commandments not to do that.

Do not want anything that belongs to someone else.
Don't want anyone's house, wife or husband,
slaves, oxen, donkeys or anything else.
EXODUS 20:17 CEV

What about you? Are there places you can't go to very often or things you see that you don't have that make you feel unhappy with what you do have? Do you look at the lives of your friends and wish your life was more like theirs? It is not easy to fight those jealous and discontent feelings sometimes. I totally get it! I have to fight them every time I think about the beach and Disney World. LOL!

But the writer named Paul in the Bible tells us the way. He said, "I am not complaining about having too little. I have learned to be satisfied with whatever I have. I know what it is to be poor or to have plenty, and I have lived under all kinds of conditions. I know what it means to be full or to be hungry, to have too much or too little. Christ gives me the strength to face anything" (Philippians 4:11–13 CEV).

Christ—*Jesus*—is the way to fight those jealous and "I want that so bad!" feelings. Focusing on Him and all that you have with Him as your Savior gives you the strength to be content with what He's given you now and trust that He'll give you all you need and also plenty of blessing on top of that.

> *It's healthy to be content,*
> *but envy can eat you up.*
> PROVERBS 14:30 CEV

> *True godliness with contentment is itself great*
> *wealth. After all, we brought nothing with us*
> *when we came into the world, and we can't take*
> *anything with us when we leave it. So if we have*
> *enough food and clothing, let us be content.*
> 1 TIMOTHY 6:6–8 NLT

*People who want to be rich fall into all sorts of
temptations and traps. They are caught by foolish and
harmful desires that drag them down and destroy them.
The love of money causes all kinds of trouble. Some
people want money so much that they have given up
their faith and caused themselves a lot of pain.*

1 Timothy 6:9–10 cev

*Don't fall in love with money. Be satisfied with
what you have. The Lord has promised that
he will not leave us or desert us.*

Hebrews 13:5 cev

*"Don't be greedy! Owning a lot
of things won't make your life safe."*

Luke 12:15 cev

*Trust in the Lord and do good. Then you will live safely
in the land and prosper. Take delight in the Lord, and he
will give you your heart's desires. Commit everything you
do to the Lord. Trust him, and he will help you.*

Psalm 37:3–5 nlt

It All Matters to Jesus

❀ Not comparing our lives with others' matters to Jesus.

❀ Not comparing our stuff with others' matters to Jesus.

❀ Not wishing you had what everyone else has matters to Jesus.

❀ Not loving money matters to Jesus.

❀ Being content and happy with what you already have matters to Jesus.

❀ Being content and happy with Him most of all matters to Jesus.

Find the Good Fruit

Have you noticed yet that being a Christian sure can get confusing sometimes? Maybe these are some of the questions you have (I know I do!):

Why do some Christians dress a certain way and others don't?

Why do some Christians watch just about any movies and TV and others watch nothing?

Why do some Christian churches have rock bands and others have only pianos and organs?

Why do some churches dunk people under water in baptism and others just sprinkle baby heads?

There are many different kinds of churches and preachers and teachers who say they are Christians but teach lots of different kinds of things. Sometimes those differences are okay because it's just a matter of tastes and opinions and traditions. But sometimes those things are not okay because they don't add up with what the Bible teaches.

In 2 Corinthians 11:13–15 (CEV), Paul says this about these false teachers: "They only pretend to be apostles of Christ. And it is no wonder. Even Satan tries to make himself look like an angel of light. So why does it seem strange for Satan's servants to pretend to do what is right? Someday they will get exactly what they deserve."

That's kinda scary, isn't it? But it doesn't have to be if we plant ourselves in Jesus and keep following Him like this scripture says:

You have accepted Christ Jesus as your Lord. Now keep on following him. Plant your roots in Christ and let him be the foundation for your life. Be strong in your faith, just as you were taught. And be grateful. Don't let anyone fool you by using senseless arguments. These arguments may sound wise, but they are only human teachings. They come from the powers of this world and not from Christ.
COLOSSIANS 2:6-8 CEV

So, how can you know what's good teaching and what's bad teaching, what's from God and what's from the world? When Jesus is your Savior, you have the Holy Spirit in you, and when you are walking closely with God and reading His Word every day, the Holy Spirit raises red flags or sounds warning bells in your brain for you when you hear things that don't match up with His Word. So always test things against God's Word. First Thessalonians 5:21-22 (CEV) says, "Put everything to the test. Accept what is good and don't have anything to do with evil."

The Bible is always, always, always your answer when things get confusing about church and being a Christian. Go to the Bible and pray and ask God to show you what is right. He wants you to be what's called *discerning*. If you're not sure what that word means, *Merriam-Webster* dictionary says *discern* means "to recognize or identify as separate and unique" as in, discerning right from wrong. God wants you to be able to recognize and identify true Christian teachings as separate and unique in that they stand strong on God's Word, no matter how unpopular they might be in the world around us.

Think of it as finding the good fruit. Just like you wouldn't keep going to a grocery store that only sold mushy brown bananas and you wouldn't get apples from an orchard that only grew apples with worms crawling out of them (EWWW!), you shouldn't go to a church that is not producing good fruit or learn from a teacher who is not producing good fruit.

The Bible says this about figuring out who is truly a follower and teacher of Jesus and who is not: "A good tree cannot produce bad fruit, and a bad tree cannot produce good fruit. Every tree that produces bad fruit will be chopped down and burned. You can tell who the false prophets are by their deeds" (Matthew 7:18–20 CEV).

Here are a few more verses to help you be discerning and find the good fruit!

But the Holy Spirit produces this kind of fruit in our lives: love, joy, peace, patience, kindness, goodness, faithfulness, gentleness, and self-control.

GALATIANS 5:22-23 NLT

Dear friends, don't believe everyone who claims to have the Spirit of God. Test them all to find out if they really do come from God. Many false prophets have already gone out into the world, and you can know which ones come from God. His Spirit says that Jesus Christ had a truly human body. But when someone doesn't say this about Jesus, you know that person has a spirit that doesn't come from God and is the enemy of Christ.

1 JOHN 4:1-3 CEV

"Look beneath the surface so you can judge correctly."
JOHN 7:24 NLT

Don't copy the behavior and customs of this world, but let God transform you into a new person by changing the way you think. Then you will learn to know God's will for you, which is good and pleasing and perfect.
ROMANS 12:2 NLT

Jesus answered, "I am the way and the truth and the life. No one comes to the Father except through me."
JOHN 14:6 NIV

For a time is coming when people will no longer listen to sound and wholesome teaching. They will follow their own desires and will look for teachers who will tell them whatever their itching ears want to hear. They will reject the truth and chase after myths. But you should keep a clear mind in every situation. Don't be afraid of suffering for the Lord. Work at telling others the Good News, and fully carry out the ministry God has given you.
2 TIMOTHY 4:3-5 NLT

It All Matters to Jesus

❄ Looking for good fruit in Christians and in churches matters to Jesus.

❄ Being discerning matters to Jesus.

❄ Staying away from false teaching matters to Jesus.

❄ Looking for teaching that matches God's Word matters to Jesus.

Be Bright, Not Blue!

Do you have any Eeyores in your life? People who are gloomy and negative and critical all the time about pretty much everything? Eeyore of *Winnie the Pooh* fame is pretty cute and lovable even if he is so blue, but real-life Eeyores aren't so much. They can be frustrating and draining and hard to be around. As Christians especially, we should never be Eeyores. Of course we all have our down times and grumpy days, but to be negative constantly goes against what the Bible says about the hope we have in an amazing and loving God.

When I'm having a rough day, just feeling like a crabby Patty for whatever reason, I try to remember two of my favorite psalms:

Why am I discouraged? Why is my heart so sad? I will put my hope in God! I will praise him again— my Savior and my God!
PSALM 43:5 NLT

This is the day the LORD has made. We will rejoice and be glad in it.
PSALM 118:24 NLT

And then I try to repeat them again and again throughout my day. Scripture is so very powerful to change our way of thinking and put our thoughts and focus on God.

Unfortunately, there are too many "Christian Eeyores," people who say they love Jesus but they seem to constantly spread doom and gloom about our dark and sinful world, rather than trying to light it up with the love and hope that comes only from knowing Jesus as Savior. The Bible says that we are the light of the world, so choose now to be a person who will brighten everything and everyone around you with hope, not spread the darkness of negativity.

Here are just a few of the many verses about the awesome hope we have in Jesus:

But those who hope in the Lord will renew their strength. They will soar on wings like eagles; they will run and not grow weary, they will walk and not be faint.
ISAIAH 40:31 NIV

*I will never give up hope or stop praising you. All day long
I will tell the wonderful things you do to save your people.*

PSALM 71:14-15 CEV

*We boast in the hope of the glory of God. Not only so,
but we also glory in our sufferings, because we know that
suffering produces perseverance; perseverance, character;
and character, hope. And hope does not put us to shame,
because God's love has been poured out into our hearts
through the Holy Spirit, who has been given to us.*

ROMANS 5:2-5 NIV

*Always be ready to give an answer when someone
asks you about your hope. Give a kind and respectful
answer and keep your conscience clear. This way you
will make people ashamed for saying bad things
about your good conduct as a follower of Christ.*

1 PETER 3:15-16 CEV

It All Matters to Jesus

❋ Being full of joy matters to Jesus.

❋ Being full of hope matters to Jesus.

❋ Letting our joy and hope come from Him matters to Jesus.

❋ Not letting our grumpy times last for long matters to Jesus.

❋ Finding joy in each day matters to Jesus.

Somewhere over the Rainbow. . .

Do you have dreams for what you want to be when you're an adult?

My dreams for my future changed quite a bit when I was young. My very first career idea, when I started to color and draw, was to be an artist. (I truly have no real talent for drawing, so it's a good thing I didn't go with that one.) Then, like you read earlier, I had big plans to be an Olympic gymnast (even though I'd never taken a class—ha!). Then I wanted to be a teacher. Then after the first time I visited Sea World, I decided Shamu was the coolest thing ever, and I absolutely wanted to be a marine biologist. Then the more I enjoyed writing, I decided I wanted to be a famous journalist. But in junior high I realized that I love Christian books so much that I wanted to edit and write for Christian publishing companies someday. And now that's what I do!

I feel very blessed that God helped me figure out exactly what I really wanted to do with my life when I was still very young—just about thirteen years old—and then I let Him keep me on a path toward that goal.

It has definitely been bumpy at times and even seemed to go *way* off course, but I kept asking for God's help and I kept walking through the doors of opportunities that He opened. And when He closed a door, I waited and looked for the next open door, always asking for Him to help me see His will for my life in each new circumstance. It hasn't been perfect, but I can look back and see again and again how God has directed me on my career path and has given me such joy along the way, even in the hard times—because I have asked Him to guide me and I have followed Him. And because I can look back and see God in my past, I know He is with me now, and I know He is always going to be in my future.

You are never too young to start asking God to help you figure out goals for your life and find a career and purpose that He has made you for. Remember that a career should never be about how much money you will make. It should be about finding what God wants for you.

You might have great career ideas and then they might change, and that's totally okay! Sometimes that's because God is showing you why that wouldn't work well for you (like me with gymnastics—LOL!). He has created you to do good works, and He will help you figure them out if you just keep on asking Him. His Word says, "For we are God's handiwork, created in Christ Jesus to do good works, which God prepared in advance for us to do" (Ephesians 2:10 NIV). Start asking now for Him to show you what those are and where they will lead you. And then never stop asking Him to help guide you.

We can make our plans,
but the Lord determines our steps.
PROVERBS 16:9 NLT

"For I know the plans I have for you," declares the Lord,
"plans to prosper you and not to harm you, plans to give
you hope and a future. Then you will call on me and come
and pray to me, and I will listen to you. You will seek me
and find me when you seek me with all your heart."
JEREMIAH 29:11–13 NIV

Trust in the Lord with all your heart and lean not on
your own understanding; in all your ways submit
to him, and he will make your paths straight.
PROVERBS 3:5-6 NIV

It All Matters to Jesus

❈ Your dreams for the future matter to Jesus.

❈ Helping you find the things God has created you to do matters to Jesus.

❈ Letting God lead you in all things matters to Jesus.

Thanksgiving All Year Long

If you could only pick one thing to eat at Thanksgiving, what would it be? Such a crazy question, right? Because Thanksgiving is a smorgasbord (isn't that word, *smorgasbord*, fun to say?) of awesome food. The turkey, the stuffing, the mashed potatoes, the sweet potatoes, the corn, and all the pie. Oh, the pie! It's pretty much impossible to pick just one favorite Thanksgiving food to eat!

I bet it's also pretty much impossible for you to think of just one thing you have to be thankful for. You probably have *lots* of things. I love that there's an entire holiday devoted to being thankful. But of course, don't ever save your thankfulness for just that one day. Develop an attitude of gratitude all year long, on every day of the year. Be thankful for the big things in your life and be thankful for the simple things, too. When you have problems and stress in your life, focus on all the blessings rather than the troubles.

Let these verses be your gratitude guide!

*Oh give thanks to the LORD, for he is good,
for his steadfast love endures forever!*

PSALM 107:1 ESV

*Make a joyful noise to the L*ORD*, all the earth!*
*Serve the L*ORD *with gladness!*
Come into his presence with singing!
*Know that the L*ORD*, he is God!*
It is he who made us, and we are his;
we are his people, and the sheep of his pasture.
Enter his gates with thanksgiving,
and his courts with praise!
Give thanks to him; bless his name!
*For the L*ORD *is good;*
his steadfast love endures forever,
and his faithfulness to all generations.

PSALM 100:1–5 ESV

Giving thanks always and for everything to God the
Father in the name of our Lord Jesus Christ.

EPHESIANS 5:20 ESV

"But giving thanks is a sacrifice that truly honors me."

PSALM 50:23 NLT

Just as you accepted Christ Jesus as your Lord, you must
continue to follow him. Let your roots grow down into
him, and let your lives be built on him. Then your faith
will grow strong in the truth you were taught, and you will
overflow with thankfulness.

COLOSSIANS 2:6–7 NLT

They were also to stand every morning to thank and praise the LORD. They were to do the same in the evening.
1 CHRONICLES 23:30 NIV

Jesus then took the loaves, and when he had given thanks, he distributed them to those who were seated.
JOHN 6:11 ESV

Thanks be to God for his inexpressible gift!
2 CORINTHIANS 9:15 ESV

Yes, you will be enriched in every way so that you can always be generous. And when we take your gifts to those who need them, they will thank God. So two good things will result from this ministry of giving—the needs of the believers in Jerusalem will be met, and they will joyfully express their thanks to God.
2 CORINTHIANS 9:11-12 NLT

Devote yourselves to prayer, being watchful and thankful.
COLOSSIANS 4:2 NIV

Always be joyful and never stop praying. Whatever happens, keep thanking God because of Jesus Christ. This is what God wants you to do.
1 THESSALONIANS 5:16-18 CEV

It All Matter to Jesus

❋ Being full of thanks matters to Jesus.

❋ Thanking God for little things matters to Jesus.

❋ Thanking God for big things matters to Jesus.

❋ Celebrating your thankfulness all year long matters to Jesus.

God and Others First

I don't hear this word used very often anymore, but *vespers* means "an evening prayer or worship service." At the church camp I went to in junior high, we had vespers—singing and praying around a campfire late at night—and it was amazing. One song I'll never forget singing during vespers in that beautiful setting was "Humble Yourself in the Sight of the Lord." It wasn't hard to feel humble out in God's amazing creation, under His big dark sky with a zillion stars that He made twinkling overhead out in big wide outer space.

Do you know what being humble or having humility means? *Merriam-Webster* says it's "not proud; not thinking of yourself as better than other people."

Being humble matters to Jesus. The Bible tells us not to be proud:

> *"God opposes everyone who is proud,*
> *but he is kind to everyone who is humble."*
> JAMES 4:6 CEV

> *Too much pride will destroy you.*
> PROVERBS 16:18 CEV

And it tells us to think of others before ourselves:

Don't be selfish; don't try to impress others.
Be humble, thinking of others as better than
yourselves. Don't look out only for your own
interests, but take an interest in others, too.
PHILIPPIANS 2:3–4 NLT

Sometimes people misunderstand *humble* and think it's just people thinking badly about themselves and not having any self-confidence. It's not that you can't have confidence, but your confidence shouldn't be in yourself; it should be in Jesus.

The Scriptures say, "If you want to brag, then brag about
the Lord." You may brag about yourself, but the only
approval that counts is the Lord's approval.
2 CORINTHIANS 10:17–18 CEV

Sometimes, being humble is all about being teachable, realizing that so many others are older and wiser and more mature than you and you can learn from them and their successes and failures, rather than always trying things on your own in your own way.

Get all the advice and instruction you can,
so you will be wise the rest of your life.
PROVERBS 19:20 NLT

Give instruction to a wise man, and he will be still wiser;
teach a righteous man, and he will increase in learning.
PROVERBS 9:9 ESV

Let the wise hear and increase in learning,
and the one who understands obtain guidance.
PROVERBS 1:5 ESV

Just as iron sharpens iron,
friends sharpen the minds
of each other.
PROVERBS 27:17 CEV

Direct your children onto the right path,
and when they are older, they will not leave it.
PROVERBS 22:6 NLT

It can be such a struggle because it's our natural way
to think of ourselves first and foremost, but ask God to
make you humble, and watch the way He will lift you up!

If you put yourself above others, you will be put down.
But if you humble yourself, you will be honored.
LUKE 14:11 CEV

The reward for humility and fear of
the LORD is riches and honor and life.
PROVERBS 22:4 ESV

It All Matters to Jesus

❋ Bragging only about God matters to Jesus.

❋ Putting others before yourself matters to Jesus.

❋ Not thinking of yourself as better than others matters to Jesus.

❋ Being teachable matters to Jesus.

❋ Not being full of pride matters to Jesus.

Growing Up

I used to HATE going to the doctor! (And I'm not all that much better about it now!) One time when I was about four years old and going in for a checkup (which I knew probably meant shots!—OUCH!), I cried hysterically and then I threw up all over the nurse. Nice, huh?

How about you? Do you like going to the doctor, or do you freak out a little? Whether you like it or not, it's good to get your health checked regularly. And when you're young, it's good to check that you're growing properly. If you've stopped growing, then there could be a serious problem.

Just like your body needs growth, so does your spirit, and the way it grows is through your relationship with God. Don't ever stop following Him, listening to Him, serving Him, and loving Him—those are the ways to keep growing in Him.

I pray that your love will keep on growing and that you will fully know and understand how to make the right choices. Then you will still be pure and innocent when Christ returns. And until that day, Jesus Christ will keep you busy doing good deeds that bring glory and praise to God.

PHILIPPIANS 1:9-11 CEV

But grow in the grace and knowledge of our Lord and Savior Jesus Christ.

2 PETER 3:18 ESV

Much more could be said about this subject. But it is hard to explain, and all of you are slow to understand. By now you should have been teachers, but once again you need to be taught the simplest things about what God has said. You need milk instead of solid food. People who live on milk are like babies who don't really know what is right. Solid food is for mature people who have been trained to know right from wrong.

HEBREWS 5:11-14 CEV

*We must try to become mature and start
thinking about more than just the basic
things we were taught about Christ.*

HEBREWS 6:1 CEV

*Like newborn babies, you must crave pure spiritual milk
so that you will grow into a full experience of salvation.
Cry out for this nourishment, now that you have
had a taste of the Lord's kindness.*

1 PETER 2:2-3 NLT

*Rather, speaking the truth in love, we are to grow up in
every way into him who is the head, into Christ.*

EPHESIANS 4:15 ESV

*We ask God to give you complete knowledge of
his will and to give you spiritual wisdom and
understanding. Then the way you live will always
honor and please the Lord, and your lives will
produce every kind of good fruit. All the while, you will
grow as you learn to know God better and better.*

COLOSSIANS 1:9-10 NLT

*Dear friends, you always followed my instructions
when I was with you. And now that I am away, it is even
more important. Work hard to show the results of your
salvation, obeying God with deep reverence and fear.
For God is working in you, giving you the desire
and the power to do what pleases him.*

PHILIPPIANS 2:12-13 NLT

It All Matters to Jesus

� Growing healthy bodies matters to Jesus.

✿ Growing in our relationship with God matters even more to Jesus.

✿ Studying God's Word matters to Jesus.

Testing, Testing. . .

I'm not a math whiz, but I liked to get good grades when I was in school, and I also liked to ace my tests no matter what subject they were in. So in my first year of college, I was in precalculus and before the end of the semester exam, I was a wreck. I wanted to get an A. I knew if I studied hard enough, I could get an A, but I was super stressed out about getting that A—so stressed that I got the most ginormous zit on my face that I think the world has ever seen. Seriously, it was bad. So gross, right?

Have you ever stressed so much over a test that you got physically sick in some way? Tests can be such a pain, but they're good for proving what we're able to do.

Life tests, meaning those tough and challenging times and situations that come into our lives—like an awful sickness or a major move away from all your friends or a job loss for one of your parents or all kinds of hard things—aren't fun, either, but they can be really good for us because they prove if our faith in God is real or not.

If someone says, "I love God and I totally trust Him" when times are good in her life, but then turns away from God in anger as soon as something goes wrong, then her "faith" didn't mean much, did it?

First Peter 1:5–7 (NLT) says, "Through your faith,

God is protecting you by his power until you receive this salvation, which is ready to be revealed on the last day for all to see. So be truly glad. There is wonderful joy ahead, even though you must endure many trials for a little while. These trials will show that your faith is genuine. It is being tested as fire tests and purifies gold—though your faith is far more precious than mere gold. So when your faith remains strong through many trials, it will bring you much praise and glory and honor on the day when Jesus Christ is revealed to the whole world."

And if we let them, spiritual tests help us grow and strengthen our faith in God, and they can show what awesome things God is able to do in and through and for us.

When troubles of any kind come your way, consider it an opportunity for great joy. For you know that when your faith is tested, your endurance has a chance to grow. So let it grow, for when your endurance is fully developed, you will be perfect and complete, needing nothing.

JAMES 1:2–4 NLT

God will bless you, if you don't give up when your faith is being tested. He will reward you with a glorious life, just as he rewards everyone who loves him.

JAMES 1:12 CEV

Dear friends, don't be surprised or shocked that you are going through testing that is like walking through fire. Be glad for the chance to suffer as Christ suffered. It will prepare you for even greater happiness when he makes his glorious return.

1 PETER 4:12–13 CEV

So don't be afraid of testing. Let the all-knowing, all-powerful God who loves you help you through every type of test you face in life.

It All Matters to Jesus

❋ The stress you feel about a test matters to Jesus.

❋ Helping you through a test matters to Jesus.

❋ Helping you grow in knowledge and maturity because of a test matters to Jesus.

❋ Proving your faith through a test matters to Jesus.

490!

Is there something you wish you could do seventy times seven times? That's a lot of times. Four hundred and ninety to be exact. (I double-checked that on a calculator, just to be sure.) I'd like to go down my very favorite amusement park ride—Splash Mountain at Disney World—490 times. Not all in the same day, of course! Probably not even all in the same year. Spreading that out over a lot of vacations to Disney would be nice. LOL!

What about forgiving? Do you think you could do that for someone 490 times? It seems like we'd get tired of forgiving a person after maybe even just five times. Peter, in the Bible, asked if seven times was enough. But Jesus said not seven, but *seventy times seven*. Wow. That's a lot. Here's the verse:

> *Then Peter came to him and asked,*
> *"Lord, how often should I forgive someone*
> *who sins against me? Seven times?"*
> *"No, not seven times," Jesus replied,*
> *"but seventy times seven!"*
> MATTHEW 18:21-22 NLT

223

So, does this mean you should keep a journal or a chart or an app on your phone to keep track of every time you've forgiven someone, and then once you hit 490, you get to be done?

No. That's not what it means. Peter was asking about seven times, and Jesus was answering in a way to show that whatever number you're thinking of forgiving, then do it seventy more times than that. In other words, go way above and beyond what's expected and just don't ever stop forgiving.

Forgiveness is so very important to Jesus. It's the whole reason He came to us—to live and die for our sin and rise again so that God could offer us forgiveness and a relationship with Him through Jesus.

God treats everyone alike. He accepts people only because they have faith in Jesus Christ. All of us have sinned and fallen short of God's glory. But God treats us much better than we deserve, and because of Christ Jesus, he freely accepts us and sets us free from our sins. God sent Christ to be our sacrifice. Christ offered his life's blood, so that by faith in him we could come to God. And God did this to show that in the past he was right to be patient and forgive sinners. This also shows that God is right when he accepts people who have faith in Jesus.
ROMANS 3:22–26 CEV

If we don't forgive, that's like telling God that His HUGE forgiveness of us doesn't actually matter so much. And the Bible tells us that's a really bad idea because there's a major consequence for that:

If you forgive others for the wrongs they do to you, your Father in heaven will forgive you. But if you don't forgive others, your Father will not forgive your sins.
MATTHEW 6:14–15 CEV

That's really serious. So don't ever stop forgiving. No matter how hard it is, no matter what wrong has been done to you, and as much as you're absolutely sure you just can't do it, ask God for help and let Him do it for and through you, in His power. Think about the way He forgives you endlessly and how awful it would be if He stopped. Let yourself fill up with thankfulness for that, and then let gratitude and forgiveness overflow from your life and into others' lives who do you wrong.

Here are some more scriptures on forgiveness to help you:

Be kind to one another, tenderhearted, forgiving one another, as God in Christ forgave you.
EPHESIANS 4:32 ESV

"And whenever you stand praying, forgive, if you have anything against anyone, so that your Father also who is in heaven may forgive you your trespasses."

MARK 11:25 ESV

Put up with each other, and forgive anyone who does you wrong, just as Christ has forgiven you. Love is more important than anything else. It is what ties everything completely together.

COLOSSIANS 3:13-14 CEV

If we confess our sins, he is faithful and just to forgive us our sins and to cleanse us from all unrighteousness. If we say we have not sinned, we make him a liar, and his word is not in us.

1 JOHN 1:9-10 ESV

He does not punish us for all our sins; he does not deal harshly with us, as we deserve. For his unfailing love toward those who fear him is as great as the height of the heavens above the earth. He has removed our sins as far from us as the east is from the west. The LORD is like a father to his children, tender and compassionate to those who fear him. For he knows how weak we are; he remembers we are only dust.

PSALM 103:10-14 NLT

It All Matters to Jesus

✳ Forgiving others matters to Jesus.

✳ Forgiving them again matters to Jesus.

✳ Remembering how much God forgives us matters to Jesus.

Obsessed

If you've ever watched the show *Phineas and Ferb*, you know that Candace is a little. . .shall we say, obsessed?. . .with her boyfriend, Jeremy. Maybe even more than just a little.

But Candace is a crazy cartoon character. Do you know anyone in real life who seems obsessed? Is there anything or anyone you're obsessed with? Sometimes people say that in a silly way, like "I'm completely obsessed with ____ [fill in the blank]," meaning they're really into or enjoy something. It's not necessarily a bad thing. We all have favorite TV shows and music and hobbies and sports and teams that we're fans of. What matters is that we don't take that hobby or interest to a level where it's the only thing we ever talk about or think about and it takes up all our time and attention. If that happens, then it becomes something that we worship, not just enjoy. It basically becomes like a god to us. And that's not good.

God, the one true God, is the only One who deserves our worship (it's even why His pronouns are capitalized when no one else's are!), and He wants to be the center of our attention because He is good and loving and amazing! Even the first two of the Ten Commandments tell us clearly to have no other gods before the one true God and not to worship anyone or anything else:

Then God gave the people all these instructions:
*"I am the L*ORD *your God, who rescued you from the land*
of Egypt, the place of your slavery. You must not have any
other god but me. You must not make for yourself an idol
of any kind or an image of anything in the heavens
or on the earth or in the sea. You must not bow down to
*them or worship them, for I, the L*ORD *your God, am a*
jealous God who will not tolerate your affection for
any other gods. I lay the sins of the parents upon their
children; the entire family is affected—even children in
the third and fourth generations of those who reject me.
But I lavish unfailing love for a thousand generations
on those who love me and obey my commands."

EXODUS 20:1–6 NLT

Other verses that talk about not being obsessed with anything but God are these:

One day an expert in religious law stood up to test Jesus by asking him this question: "Teacher, what should I do to inherit eternal life?" Jesus replied, "What does the law of Moses say? How do you read it?" The man answered, " 'You must love the Lord your God with all your heart, all your soul, all your strength, and all your mind.' And, 'Love your neighbor as yourself.' " "Right!" Jesus told him. "Do this and you will live!"

LUKE 10:25-28 NLT

If then you have been raised with Christ, seek the things that are above, where Christ is, seated at the right hand of God.

COLOSSIANS 3:1 ESV

"No one can serve two masters. For you will hate one and love the other; you will be devoted to one and despise the other. You cannot serve both God and money."

LUKE 16:13 NLT

Then Jesus said to him, "Be gone, Satan! For it is written, 'You shall worship the Lord your God and him only shall you serve.' "

MATTHEW 4:10 ESV

Do not conform to the pattern of this world,
but be transformed by the renewing of your mind.
Then you will be able to test and approve what
God's will is—his good, pleasing and perfect will.

ROMANS 12:2 NIV

So be careful what you're "into" and how much you're into it. Make sure you're not so into it that you put it before God and your relationship with Him. It's hard, I know! There are so many cool things in the world that seem harmless, and they suck us in and steal our attention and enthusiasm. So, every day, ask God to be first and most important in your life. Let Him fill your thoughts, and do everything with Him in mind. Live a life so that everyone who knows you can say that you are obsessed with only this—loving and living for God in Jesus!

It All Matters to Jesus

❅ Worshipping only the one true God matters to Jesus.

❅ Not having any other gods matters to Jesus.

❅ Not being obsessed with anything or anyone but God matters to Jesus.

❅ Serving only God matters to Jesus.

❅ Letting God be the center of our love and attention matters to Jesus.

Truth Trumps Feelings

Have you ever played a card game where there are trump cards that always win the hand? Well, let's talk about how truth always trumps our feelings. We've talked about feelings a lot so far, feelings of anger, frustration, sadness, joy. And all your feelings matter to Jesus because He cares so much about you. But something incredibly important for you to learn and remember through every single season of your life is that feelings can sometimes blind you to the truth, and feelings are never more important than the truth.

For example:

You might feel happy when disobeying your parents because you're doing what your friends wanted you to do, but here's the truth—it's still wrong to disobey your parents.

Children, obey your parents because you belong to the Lord, for this is the right thing to do.
EPHESIANS 6:1 NLT

You might feel like it's so yummy to eat a whole huge bag of M&M'S in one sitting and then wash it down with a Mountain Dew because you love the taste, but here's the truth—all that sugar at once is totally not good for your body, and there's a good chance it's going to make you sick.

Don't you realize that your body is the temple of the Holy Spirit, who lives in you and was given to you by God? You do not belong to yourself, for God bought you with a high price. So you must honor God with your body.

1 Corinthians 6:19–20 nlt

So, whether you eat or drink, or whatever you do, do all to the glory of God.

1 Corinthians 10:31 esv

You might feel crazy angry if your little brother does something to ruin your stuff that you told him not to touch, but don't forget the truth—you love him, and your relationship matters more than whatever was ruined.

Don't be selfish; don't try to impress others. Be humble, thinking of others as better than yourselves. Don't look out only for your own interests, but take an interest in others, too.

Philippians 2:3–4 nlt

Most important of all, continue to show deep love
for each other, for love covers a multitude of sins.
1 PETER 4:8 NLT

You might feel like life is SO unfair and your parents
must hate you because they say you can't go to the
sleepover that everyone else is going to, but here's the
truth—your parents love you and want what's best for you,
and you need to trust their reasons for not letting you go.

Pay attention to your father, and don't
neglect your mother when she grows old.
PROVERBS 23:22 CEV

Children with good sense accept correction from their
parents, but stubborn children ignore it completely.
PROVERBS 13:1 CEV

My child, obey the teachings of your parents,
and wear their teachings as you would a
lovely hat or a pretty necklace.
PROVERBS 1:8-9 CEV

You might feel like you hate doing daily chores or
following rules your parents set, but here's the truth—you
need discipline for all kinds of things later in life, and
if your parents are teaching you that now, then they
obviously love you.

*Those who spare the rod of discipline hate
their children. Those who love their children
care enough to discipline them.*
PROVERBS 13:24 NLT

*Correct your children, and they will be wise;
children out of control disgrace their mothers.*
PROVERBS 29:15 CEV

*Our human fathers correct us for a short time, and they
do it as they think best. But God corrects us for our
own good, because he wants us to be holy, as he is.
It is never fun to be corrected. In fact, at the time it is
always painful. But if we learn to obey by being
corrected, we will do right and live at peace.*
HEBREWS 12:10–11 CEV

*My child, don't reject the LORD's discipline, and don't be
upset when he corrects you. For the LORD corrects those he
loves, just as a father corrects a child in whom he delights.*
PROVERBS 3:11–12 NLT

You might feel like God has forgotten you when
you're in a horrible situation, but here's the truth:

*God has said, "Never will I leave you;
never will I forsake you."*
HEBREWS 13:5 NIV

You may feel like the Bible is not true, but here's the truth:

For the word of God is alive and powerful. It is sharper than the sharpest two-edged sword, cutting between soul and spirit, between joint and marrow. It exposes our innermost thoughts and desires.

HEBREWS 4:12 NLT

Since childhood, you have known the Holy Scriptures that are able to make you wise enough to have faith in Christ Jesus and be saved. Everything in the Scriptures is God's Word. All of it is useful for teaching and helping people and for correcting them and showing them how to live.

2 TIMOTHY 3:15-16 CEV

Your word is a lamp to my feet and a light to my path.

PSALM 119:105 ESV

"Heaven and earth will pass away, but my words will not pass away."

MARK 13:31 ESV

Knowing this first of all, that no prophecy of Scripture comes from someone's own interpretation. For no prophecy was ever produced by the will of man, but men spoke from God as they were carried along by the Holy Spirit.

2 PETER 1:20-21 ESV

There will be times you don't feel like being a Christian, that it would be easier to just be like the world, but here's the truth:

Do not love this world nor the things it offers you, for when you love the world, you do not have the love of the Father in you. For the world offers only a craving for physical pleasure, a craving for everything we see, and pride in our achievements and possessions. These are not from the Father, but are from this world. And this world is fading away, along with everything that people crave. But anyone who does what pleases God will live forever.
1 JOHN 2:15–17 NLT

So when your feelings might be overtaking you, remind yourself in all situations to step back and think about what is true. No matter how strong your feelings are, they will lie to you sometimes, and the truth always trumps them. And the truth is always found in God's Word.

It All Matters to Jesus

❋ All of your feelings matter to Jesus.

❋ Realizing that your feelings can lead you the wrong way matters to Jesus.

❋ Focusing on the truth over your feelings matters to Jesus.

Your ID

There is a lot of talk these days about identity—who you are and your beliefs and feelings about yourself. Some of it is good talk, and some of it not so much—meaning a lot of what's being said about identity in our culture today starts to get confusing and contradictory to God's Word.

So be careful and be discerning like we talked about earlier. The most important thing to know about your identity is not what your family and friends and society think about you. It's not even what you *feel* about yourself. (Remember, truth always trumps feelings!)

The most important question to ask yourself about your identity is, who did God create you to be?

And the more you keep following Him and seeking Him through His Word and through prayer, the more He will keep showing that to you.

Here are truths from the Bible about who you really are:

So God created human beings in his own image.
In the image of God he created them;
male and female he created them.

GENESIS 1:27 NLT

None of these was the right kind of partner for the man.
So the LORD God made him fall into a deep sleep, and
he took out one of the man's ribs. Then after closing the
man's side, the LORD made a woman out of the rib.
The LORD God brought her to the man,
and the man exclaimed,
"Here is someone like me! She is part of my body,
my own flesh and bones. She came from me, a man.
So I will name her Woman!"
That's why a man will leave his own father and mother.
He marries a woman, and the two of them
become like one person.

GENESIS 2:20-24 CEV

"I knew you before I formed
you in your mother's womb."

JEREMIAH 1:5 NLT

For we are God's handiwork, created in Christ Jesus to do
good works, which God prepared in advance for us to do.

EPHESIANS 2:10 NIV

Anyone who belongs to Christ has become a new person.
The old life is gone; a new life has begun!
2 CORINTHIANS 5:17 NLT

Let the Spirit change your way of thinking and make
you into a new person. You were created to be like God,
and so you must please him and be truly holy.
EPHESIANS 4:23-24 CEV

God's Spirit doesn't make us slaves who are afraid of him.
Instead, we become his children and call him our Father.
God's Spirit makes us sure that we are his children.
ROMANS 8:15-16 CEV

Put on then, as God's chosen ones, holy and beloved,
compassionate hearts, kindness, humility,
meekness, and patience.
COLOSSIANS 3:12 ESV

I praise you, for I am fearfully and wonderfully made.
Wonderful are your works; my soul knows it very well.
PSALM 139:14 ESV

See what great love the Father has lavished on us, that we
should be called children of God! And that is what we are!
1 JOHN 3:1 NIV

Whenever you might feel confused about your identity or your purpose or who you are, just go to the One who made you and ask Him for His guidance in His Word. He made you and He loves you and He knows everything about you and who He created you to be.

You are the one who put me together
inside my mother's body, and I praise you
because of the wonderful way you created me.
Everything you do is marvelous! Of this I have no doubt.
Nothing about me is hidden from you!
I was secretly woven together deep in the earth below,
but with your own eyes you saw my body being formed.
Even before I was born, you had written in
your book everything I would do.
PSALM 139:13-16 CEV

It All Matters to Jesus

❀ Your identity matters to Jesus.

❀ Realizing that God made everything about you
matters to Jesus.

❀ Finding your identity in God matters to Jesus.

Never, Ever, Ever Give Up!

If you're here at the end of this book, I'm glad you didn't give up on it! Hopefully, you've learned more about how much you matter to Jesus, how much *every tiny detail* of your life matters to Him. Even if you truly know that, unfortunately there will still be days you are going to feel like giving up on Him. There will be days when you're tired of waiting on Him to come through for that person or need you've been praying for. There will be days when it seems like it would be better to do all the selfish things the world does rather than trying to be kind and fair and put others first. There will be days when cheating seems like a great idea because studying is so hard and lots of other people cheat and don't get caught. There will be days when giving up on being a Christian seems like the smart thing to do.

But perseverance (that means not quitting even when things are hard) matters to Jesus, and you have to tell yourself now and every day that you will never, ever, *ever* give up!

You need to remember that you're in the middle of a war, a spiritual battle for souls, just like the Bible says:

We are not fighting against humans. We are fighting against forces and authorities and against rulers of darkness and powers in the spiritual world. So put on all the armor that God gives. Then when that evil day comes, you will be able to defend yourself. And when the battle is over, you will still be standing firm.
Be ready! Let the truth be like a belt around your waist, and let God's justice protect you like armor. Your desire to tell the good news about peace should be like shoes on your feet. Let your faith be like a shield, and you will be able to stop all the flaming arrows of the evil one. Let God's saving power be like a helmet, and for a sword use God's message that comes from the Spirit.
Never stop praying, especially for others. Always pray by the power of the Spirit. Stay alert and keep praying for God's people.
EPHESIANS 6:12–18 CEV

You have an enemy trying so hard every day to make you quit:

Stay alert! Watch out for your great enemy, the devil. He prowls around like a roaring lion, looking for someone to devour. Stand firm against him, and be strong in your faith. Remember that your family of believers all over the world is going through the same kind of suffering you are.
1 PETER 5:8–9 NLT

Don't let the enemy win! God is GREATER than these things, and He wins the war!

"I have told you all this so that you may have peace in me. Here on earth you will have many trials and sorrows. But take heart, because I have overcome the world."
JOHN 16:33 NLT

The God of peace will soon crush Satan under your feet.
ROMANS 16:20 ESV

And while it does seem sometimes like He's taking FOREVER to make good on His promises, you have to be patient because:

Dear friends, don't forget that for the Lord one day is the same as a thousand years, and a thousand years is the same as one day. The Lord isn't slow about keeping his promises, as some people think he is. In fact, God is patient, because he wants everyone to turn from sin and no one to be lost.

The day of the Lord's return will surprise us like a thief. The heavens will disappear with a loud noise, and the heat will melt the whole universe. Then the earth and everything on it will be seen for what they are. Everything will be destroyed. So you should serve and honor God by the way you live. You should look forward to the day when God judges everyone, and you should try to make it come soon. On that day the heavens will be destroyed by fire, and everything else will melt in the heat. But God has promised us a new heaven and a new earth, where justice will rule. We are really looking forward to that!

My friends, while you are waiting, you should make certain that the Lord finds you pure, spotless, and living at peace. Don't forget that the Lord is patient because he wants people to be saved.

2 PETER 3:8-15 CEV

If you're an athlete who likes to run, then these verses will really encourage you:

Such a large crowd of witnesses is all around us! So we must get rid of everything that slows us down, especially the sin that just won't let go. And we must be determined to run the race that is ahead of us. We must keep our eyes on Jesus, who leads us and makes our faith complete. He endured the shame of being nailed to a cross, because he knew that later on he would be glad he did. Now he is seated at the right side of God's throne! So keep your mind on Jesus, who put up with many insults from sinners. Then you won't get discouraged and give up.
HEBREWS 12:1–3 CEV

But some of us aren't athletes, so think about it this way: If you truly love to make music, you don't give up till you've mastered the piece and can play it with ease.

If you truly love to dance, you don't give up till you've memorized every step and perform them effortlessly.

If you truly love to make art, you don't give up till you've completed your masterpiece.

If you truly love video games, you don't give up till you've conquered every level of your favorite game.

You get the idea.

And if you truly love Jesus and know that you matter to Him, you don't give up on following Him and following His Word. Not ever.

Jesus came once—He lived and died and rose again to show you how much you matter to Him, to save you from your sin—and He is coming back.

Make sure you catch that: He IS COMING BACK!

Take courage, take heart, keep your head up, don't give up—and one day you'll be standing before Him, and you'll hear Him say, "Well done. . ." (see Matthew 25:23).

Let us not become weary in doing good, for at the proper time we will reap a harvest if we do not give up.
GALATIANS 6:9 NIV

It All Matters to Jesus

� Realizing that God is patient because He wants as many people as possible to be saved matters to Jesus.

✤ Not growing tired of doing good matters to Jesus.

✤ Fighting the enemy who is trying to destroy us matters to Jesus.

✤ Never giving up on God matters to Jesus.

Dear Jesus, please keep each girl who has read this book so very close to You. Let her see how incredibly much You love her! Help her to seek You always, through the Bible and through prayer and through serving You. Please give her wisdom and guide her in Your ways to make choices that honor You, even when those right choices are hard and so different from the world around her. Please bless her in amazing ways and help her to shine brightly and confidently for You, sharing Your love so that others want to know You as their Savior, too. Thank You, thank You, thank You that everything matters to You, Jesus!
In Your awesome name, amen.

Scripture Index

OLD TESTAMENT

NEW TESTAMENT